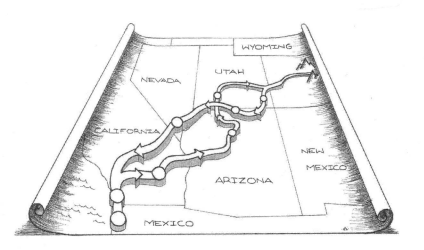

Paper Maps, No Apps

An Unplugged Travel Adventure

Johnny Welsh

Paper Maps, No Apps: An Unplugged Travel Adventure
by Johnny Welsh
Copyright © 2019 Johnny Welsh
Published by Peak 1 Publishing, LLC
PO Box 2046, Frisco, CO 80443

Photos: Kristy Smith and Johnny Welsh
Illustrations: Elle Malone
Cover design: Nick Zelinger, NZ Graphics
Publishing Team: Bublish, Inc.
ISBN: 978-0-9963078-9-5 (Print)
ISBN: 978-0-9963078-5-7 (e-Pub)
Library of Congress Control Number: 2018935797
First Edition
Printed in the United States of America

www.JohnnyWelsh.com

Contents

This book is dedicated to other books—the old-fashioned ones with paper pages in them.

Reflections from Johnny

"Yeah, uh-huh, mm-hmm, yep, yes, yeah..."

I am so tired of hearing this.

"Yeah, uh-huh, mm-hmm, yep, yes, yeah..."

That's the sound of someone pretending to answer you while mesmerized by their smartphone (or similar device) even though you're standing right next to them.

"Yeah, uh-huh, mm-hmm, yep, yes, yeah..."

Automated response system engaged. Autopilot. Mechanical nodding. Mind absent. In other words, not listening.

I know I'm not the only one noticing it. The disconnect in face-to-face interactions keeps growing; I see it happening more as smartphones get "smarter." Smarter than...? I wonder, will smartphones and social media be the biggest distractors of interpersonal communications in our lifetime? I mean, could it be the end of "Hello"?

I've been a professional bartender of twenty-five years. Not just once, but dozens of times a day, the bar will be full of people, and not one is looking up or engaging in old-fashioned conversation! Their eyes are glued to flat screens of "smartdom." Isn't the point of sitting at a bar to be social?

I imagine what would happen if aliens landed on Earth and observed us. They might think a smartphone is something we need to live, like a heart or external nervous system. I picture the baseball stadium beer guys yelling, "Get your umbilical cords here!" while holding up a nutritious dish of technology with a side of gigabytes.

I wonder if those little screens control our next moves—all of our moves—in our lives. Anyone read 1984? Big brother doesn't need to watch anymore. He has more info than could possibly be used. We have volunteered our biographies via public profiles to see if they mattered. The lure was too tempting to resist. It's no longer just a carrot on a stick. We can't live without constant affirmation our lives are thumbs-up, and it's worse for the younger generations. I can't imagine growing up in today's world. Even if you wanted to rebel against such a social force, you would risk too much, according to an impressionable mind: you would risk becoming invisible.

I looked a little deeper. This growing reliance on mobile technology and devices is actually impacting our brains. In The Shallows: What the Internet is Doing to Our Brains, Nicholas Carr explains the impact on the brain's neuroplasticity. Technology use is changing our neurological wiring, how we think and interpret data. It's like app creators know our brains crave random pop-up information and scattered topics.

In a recent NPR interview, Adam Alter noted the human attention span has decreased from twelve seconds to eight seconds in the past dozen or so years. This is the same time frame that iPhones, tablets, and the like became mainstream. I think his book title sums it up: Irresistible: The Rise of

Addictive Technology and the Business of Keeping Us Hooked.

Alter suggests the architects of these platforms take a type of Hippocratic Oath where, like doctors, they pledge to do no harm. He hints some companies have a bottom line tied to time on device. Casinos, for example, track gamblers and their time on machines. That makes me wonder: if the gaming commission regulates what is approved for gamblers, who regulates what is approved for app users?

Hollywood uses a similar tactic. The cliffhanger platform Netflix uses keeps us watching episodes the same way app designers keep us looking at our devices. Remember those analogies on standard aptitude tests? Cliffhanger platform : binge watching :: app design : excessive time on smartphone

Was I Pavlov's dog, too?

I knew, of course, I was just as guilty as those people "yeah, uh-huh," and "mm-hmm"-ing at me. When I wasn't working, I, too, had my head buried in my phone, even when my friends and loved ones were trying to get my response. Just like Pavlov's dog, I was (and still am) conditioned.

Whenever we hear a ding, we know something needs to be done: check the oven, answer the phone, or open the door. In today's world, though, we look to our devices: see who just messaged on Facebook, respond to the email that just arrived, or look at the new pictures posted. I'm salivating just thinking about it. How fast would you rate your response time to dings? I knew I was guilty of being overly obedient to the alerts. My phone would say, "Jump," I'd ask, "How high?"

"Dingifying" the world one cellular customer at a time, one puppet at a time, who are the puppet masters and why are they fighting for our attention? I bet there's an algorithm that correlates minutes of attention time to a sale of some sort.

Paper Maps, No Apps (Thank you AAA for supplying the maps.)

After I got over being annoyed and then past the dread that arose when I started researching, I took a more realistic look at smartphones in my life. I realized I was missing live opportunities to connect with people and the strange serendipities you notice when you are paying attention. I missed long, quiet afternoons outdoors. I remembered listening to the full song of a cicada as a child. Imagine having the free time to sit and listen to a singing cricket! I wanted to pay close attention to how different life could be without the constant seduction of the flat screen. Moreover, I wanted to examine my habits with a sense of humor.

So, I decided to try something outlandish: an unplugged road trip! It was time to peruse the world without smart technology: no Trip Advisor to find the next hotel, no Yelp to dig up the dirt on a restaurant, and no Siri or Alexa or even a nameless Google voice telling me when to turn left or right.

It's just me, my girlfriend, some luggage, and a lot of attitude. We're snapping our fingers!

For sixteen days, we lived on the road, detached from social media and smartphones, while navigating several states and one foreign country. We created rules, and allowed ourselves a little license:

- We used technology to locate and book a few destinations prior to departure to give our trip a basic shape, but we relied on paper maps and the whims of the road to fill our days and nights.

- I checked business emails once per morning for my pending radio show interviews.

- Kristy used her Nikon camera for the majority of photos, and I used my phone as a camera for a select few (but did not post photos until we retuned). We texted our moms every few days to let them know we were alive. In my case, it was obligatory. Little Italian mothers specialize in guilt trips if you leave them alone too long and may even send out search parties.

Our goal was to be at least 95% unplugged; and, for most of those sixteen days, we were completely old-school. We would sit and be idle, and that was okay. We even talked to each other like stagecoach days. Sometimes we would read or write.

I wrote every day on our journey, documenting my attempts to regress (or is it progress?). In the end, I had written this book. Oh, I must mention that since this was also our end-of-season vacation, we fully celebrated happy hour most days.

Keeping Serendipity Alive

Paper Maps, No Apps: An Unplugged Travel Adventure was integral to the project from the start. I hoped documenting our journey would help my readers find a balance in this faster than light and brave new world.

I wanted to record the journey in a lighthearted way and show we can still have fun without technology and make fun of our own habits. I'll be the first to admit it takes a conscious effort on my part not to be manipulated by the temptation in my hand. This book will serve as my constant reminder to be present. It's my own to-do list. High on the list are:

- **Stay balanced.** I hope to be personally vigilant about balancing my time in the natural interpersonal world with my time connecting through technology. I am not preaching total abstinence. Technology breaks may mean something different to each of us, but balance is the essence of an enriched life.
- **Read.** My attention span for reading print and e-books keeps shortening; but I know that the more I read, the more I'll get my reading brain back. Since it is almost inevitable to get caught up in the maelstrom

of distraction technology, there is a pressing need to counter this power. The act of reading a physical book quiets and calms us and allows us to become part of the story in a way no quick pop-up headline can. I do like e-books and digital readers, but the experience of a physical book incorporates the sense of touch and smell. Have you ever picked up a new book and sniffed the pages while flipping through?

- **Meditate.** Another practice to counter-balance constant distraction and disruption is meditation. In my opinion, it will top the list in years to come. In terms of quieting the mind and experiencing many physical benefits, too, it is second to none. Through meditation, you can achieve focus, which is the polar opposite of distraction.

Enough of the Technological Zombie Talk!

I hope you'll find some great ideas in these pages; but, most of all, I hope you'll laugh with me at ourselves and our world. I find it hilarious there is even a need for a cleanse like this in the first place, but enough of the scary technology zombie apocalypse talk. Are you ready to have some fun? Sit back, turn these pages, and join us on our simple journey. Here's what life can look like without smart devices.

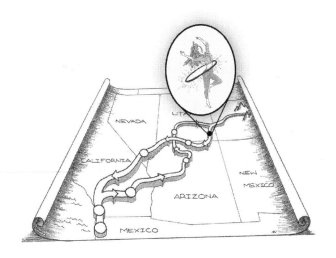

Day One
Vanishing Point

"In such a time, opting to pause and reflect, rather than panic or withdraw, is a necessity. It is not a luxury or a distraction—it is a way to increase the odds that you'll better understand, and engage productively with, the world around you."
—Thomas L. Friedman,
Thank You for Being Late

May 1, 2017
Destination: Moab, Utah

We're off!
Audiobooks in hand.
Food and water within copilot's reach.
Phones powered down and stashed out of sight.

The unfolding-of-the-map ritual begins, to be performed what feels like hundreds of times per day. Each time, it feels vital. Each time, the paper puts up a fight. We learn very quickly that paper maps don't like to be refolded. I had imagined it would be easy, collapsing like a string of paper dolls. It is not.

Kristy and I study the map for the first time sitting in our own driveway, even though we are about to take the highway we've traveled on a thousand times and know exactly where we're going for the next few hours. We are overwhelmed with excitement. These are fun times!

I can't believe it—we haven't even left the house and we're already interacting more than usual. We're both talking a mile a minute with smart technology removed from the equation, replaced by an ancient form of communication known as conversation.

 TIP If this trip inspires you to try something similar, pick a system for unplugging that works for you and your lifestyle. Keep it realistic and fun. Aim for an amount of time that makes you feel somewhat uncomfortable. We promise you'll be just fine at the end of your technology fast and live to talk about it! Visit JohnnyWelsh.com for adventure ideas and templates.

Grand Junction, Colorado

Our first stop is Grand Junction, Colorado, three hours from our house. We fuel up and buy some supplies for the campground in Moab,

Utah (still an hour ahead of us). We are now out in the scary real world where you actually have to talk to people, detached from our second brain: Google.

"Excuse me, sir? Would you happen to know where there's a Walmart nearby?" I ask an older gentleman filling his tank.

"If you're heading south, the best way is to make a left on Seventh Avenue, then a right on North. There's one on that road," he replies with a smile.

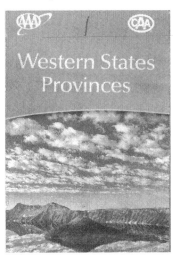

This is our map from AAA.

A real smile! Imagine that! I am witnessing a living, moving, talking emoji. Did I see a thumbs up from this man or am I stuck in text world?

"I'm in the middle of moving, so I have all this damn junk in my car," he continues casually, as if he's on the beach shooting the breeze. He sounds like William Burroughs, the old famous author/actor with a discernible high-pitched-old-man-voice.

"You wouldn't happen to have any junk that we could burn in our campfire?" I joke. Kristy, sitting in the car, windows down and within ear shot, overhears and we all laugh.

Wow, a live encounter with another human, and he doesn't have his phone either! This social experiment is happening! It's almost too good to be true. There is a world still out there.

Our only stick note guide.

After our stop, we feel it's time to film the first segment describing our themed trip: Paper Maps, No Apps.

With two bundles of firewood in hand and a full tank of gas, we are back on the highway, following the directions I had scribbled under an old grocery list on a sticky note. This relic is all we have to guide us to the campsite that a friend, Hannah, booked in Moab, Utah, for us and our other friends. "Utah. Moab. Campground. Orange tent. Find it."

Cisco, Utah

Soon after we cross the Utah state line, we see "Vanishing Point" spray-painted on an object we don't recognize, marking the entrance to Cisco, an old ghost town. We can't resist; it's almost too fitting. We are about to vanish as well, or at least we feel like we are. We have to explore.

A quick photo shoot of our vanishing point.

We pull off the highway, park on the side of the road, get out of the car, and walk around the town. Graffiti covers the dilapidated buildings and abandoned vehicles, and we're free to admire the sometimes beautiful and frequently strange art.

I feel a weight lifting from my shoulders. I'm curious about what I see. It is relaxing to have the time to walk and explore. This is our portal—our wardrobe—to a parallel world; this is our vanishing point.

Just us.

As we investigate further, we find a missing persons wall, filled with flyers and photocopied pictures of all shapes and sizes, inside one of the buildings. When the wind whips through the broken windows, the photos seem to come to life. It gives us both chills; it's like looking in a serial killer's den and seeing his collection of obsessions. I think of Jeffrey Dahmer's menu board. We are definitely creeped out. My mind likes to compound these situations and now I'm thinking about putting the lotion in the basket as we continue to explore.

I decide to see if I can scare Kristy and make her think someone is behind her.

When we return from our trip, we learn Cisco is one of the most iconic ghost towns in America. The sign that grabbed our attention refers to the cult movie Vanishing Point, filmed partly there. Other movies, most famously Thelma and Louise, contain scenes filmed there as well. On a darker note, Cisco is known for shots occasionally fired near disrespectful tourists by the few reclusive residents who still inhabit the town.

"What are you doing there? Oh my God!" I shout, looking in terror over her shoulder. Her skin puckers into goosebumps, and she runs out of the building. Great success!

Outside, as we recover from the sprint, the first of many trains roars by. Kristy captures some nice photos.

On the road to Moab

We drive with the windows down, en route to the campground. The road, with hills galore, is like a roller coaster. The topography around us changes from plateaus to buttes. The rock color deepens, reminding me of a Mars landscape photo.

Kristy and Johnny's 5 Fun Facts

1. The name Moab refers to a biblical kingdom at the edge of Zion. Early Mormon settlers may have felt they were at the edge of their world, so far from Salt Lake City, which was their city of Zion.
2. The name Utah comes from the Ute language, meaning people of the mountains.
3. Butch Cassidy and his Wild Bunch gang, known for robberies, frequently had shootouts with Moab's lawmen. Their Robbers Roost hideout was in a wild maze of canyons east of town.
4. There was a Uranium mining boom in 1952 that caused the area's population to triple. A man named Charlie Steen struck it rich by discovering the Mi Vida Uranium bonanza and became an overnight multimillionaire.
5. Today, Moab is known for mountain biking, especially in the Slickrock Canyon area.

This is a good spot for a PB&J and cold beer.

7

Campground in Moab, Utah

Unable to call Hannah for directions, we must rely on my sticky note scribbles. "Exit 214, Upper Union Creek (actually Onion Creek but I spelled it wrong; part of the journey's mystique), Hwy. 128, Camp #8." I'm sure hoping there wasn't a recent sale on orange tents!

Orange tent.

Find it.

We do!

Miraculously, we spy the orange tent tucked away in a back corner. Good ole Hannah and her directions! We get our tent up in no time and change into our relaxation gear: flip-flops, shorts, and T-shirts.

I work with Hannah at a restaurant in Frisco; I tend bar, and she's the cocktail waitress. Every chance I get, I torture her with fake spiders and bugs. She's fun to work with.

Jeremy is her fiancé, and Jason is his twin brother. (Trying to pretend I know which one I'm talking to really interferes with my late-night drinking.) Jackie is Jason's girlfriend, and she can sure sing. This is our group for the night. Or so we think...

Enter Hannah, Jeremy, Jason, and Jackie. "Did you guys see Zack by any chance?"

"Zack?" Kristy and I ponder, confused.

It turns out there's another—missing—member of our crew. Zack, whose truck is parked nearby, hasn't been seen since he told the group he was going on a short hike an hour or two before Kristy and I arrived. Ironically, nobody can call him because there's no reception. We aren't really worried yet, though.

We help each other unload what we need from our cars and begin to prep the fire pit for the evening's festivities. We catch up on our day's adventures as I explain a new campfire structure I learned on my recent trip to Italy. Randall, a man I met at a castle there, had shown me a Jenga-like tower of firewood with the kindling on top. The theory is the fire will burn down slowly, and you shouldn't have to mess with it

Do not try this at home; geniuses only!

the whole evening. Well, I learned this method with a few glasses of wine in me, so I don't exactly recall how to build it. Our attempt burns down to ash within twenty minutes.

We laugh and formulate theories as to what went wrong.

"Too much air!" I yell over and over, but that theory is ignored. Either they aren't listening or they're laughing too hard at me. I'm thinking we're pretty lucky my leaning tower of firewood didn't fall over and set our chairs afire.

Has anyone seen Zack?

We make dinner at dusk, the standard camping headlamps affixed to our heads, blinding each other at every glance. We each contribute something to dinner. The twin brothers produce a feast complete with Colorado wild game sausages, sweet potatoes, steamed broccoli, zucchini and squash. It is a meal that lives on in the savory section of the brain. Wherever that may be. I bring olive oil I helped harvest at the castle in Italy. Jeremy and Jason describe the flavor profiles they're experiencing from the fresh pressed olives. Fine culinary explanations are requisite during these elite camping moments.

Zack! Where are you?

Now it's dark, and it has been seven hours since he ventured out.

I think it will be funny to quote The Blair Witch Project, and begin yelling, "Tell me where you are Josh." Jason and Jeremy laugh at first, but we soon realize it may not be funny. After all, we are camping in the wilderness.

The Search Party

We decide to form a search party. I make sure we have all the necessary supplies: the dog, for increased senses; an LED light up Hula-Hoop as a beacon; one full bottle of wine for balance; a few beers for hydration; and tequila for bright ideas. Now, we are ready for the search!

As we yell into the night, the darkness swallows our voices; not even echoes return. The

Can a rainbow LED Hula-Hoop save a life?

wine is helping me think. I suggest we all shine our lights in the direction of the last noise heard and blink them to become a unified beacon. That lasts a whole fifteen seconds as we all hear noises from every direction. We abandon unity and shine our lights every which way.

"Yo!" we hear in the distance.

Our lights hone in on the shout. Then... nothing. We wait and offer reasons why we only heard one shout. Now it is getting a bit scary. Then we hear, "Yo!" again, louder this time.

Jeremy sprints into the darkness to find his childhood friend and disappears into the night. Earlier, he had assured us Zack knew his way around the wild and was probably okay; but on a night this dark, we knew he needed at least a little guidance. We make a chain of human lights, each of us standing about fifty yards from the next, with the rainbow Hula-Hoop as our anchor. We will guide them out of the darkness to the long-ago-burned-out fire.

"He's okay!" Jeremy shouts, and we're all relieved. He really had been lost. He had wandered off course, and although he was close by, he could not find the campground as night fell. Our shouts and lights actually helped! The twenty-minute fire did not.

Now we can drink without feeling guilty. Bottles of tequila, wine, vodka and random beers are passed around. At first, most of us choose one kind of beverage, planning to stick with it. By the end of the evening, though, we each succeed in drinking all four varieties. What an accomplishment!

The guitars come out; the singing starts. It's our own private concert. Jeremy and Jason play, and Hannah and Jackie sing. Kristy is the on-site Hula-Hoop specialist, filling the campsite with rainbows of LED light. Zack is quiet, recovering from his ordeal, drinking plenty of much-needed water. The festivities carry on into the night, not a cell phone in sight.

The next morning, we spill out of our tents rubbing our heads and laughing at the previous night's escapades. Kristy and I pack up the tent and gear, load the car, and hit the road.

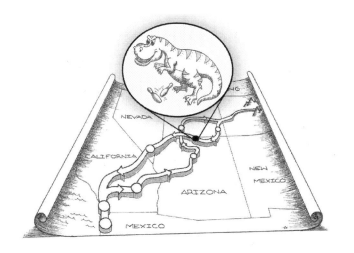

Day Two
The Seven Wonders

"Ever since I lost my phone, I feel like my other
senses have (kind of) heightened."
—Professor Shelly Oberon,
Jumanji: Welcome to the Jungle, 2017

May 2, 2017
Destination: Page, Arizona

Today's goal is to find and book a tour of Antelope
Canyon in Page, Arizona. We hit the highway
and drive for a few hours, then pull over at a T
intersection rest stop to use the facilities, refill our
water bottles, and plan the remainder of our route
for the day.

We take out our trusty paper map. It's still in good shape: no rips or tears. We're turning onto a new highway from here for the next few hours' drive. This feels exciting and relaxing at the same time. We don't have a care in the world, and new adventures await on the unfamiliar path.

Our first discovery on the way to the canyons is a big hole at the bottom of a cliff, clearly labeled in huge painted letters. "HOLE N" THE ROCK," it reads, with a giant white arrow pointing to the hole. That's all we need to fill our minds with dirty jokes—and amazement—at the spectacle. We can see there's a gift shop, but we decide not to stop.

Who wants to go see a hole in the rock?

After we get home, we learn the hole is a cave with a fully furnished home inside. People lived there for decades; it became a popular tourist attraction, even while they still lived in it! We didn't need to know all that to get a great laugh out of it, probably just like most people traveling that part of road—those who don't have their heads buried in electronic devices, that is!

With the phones away, we're much more aware of the landscape and unique objects we pass. Observations like, "Oh, look at that cool school bus all decorated as someone's house!" or "That's a funny road sign!" have replaced the dings of our cell phones and the silence that followed as we checked them. Now, we joke about peculiar sights. We share the present journey, living in the moment. With nothing else competing for our attention, we are relaxed and enjoy each other's company.

Blanding, Utah

The seemingly endless highways on every road trip are dotted with little towns along the way. These are the gems across scenic drives. Most have at least one basic tourist attraction: a good restaurant, ice cream stand, or museum.

The disconnect from technology makes us more receptive, I think, to visiting the unexpected draws. After passing by the Hole N" the Rock earlier, our appetite for the extraordinary is sharpened; so, when we see roadside signs to a dinosaur museum, we decide to follow them. I've

There is no resisting a purchase for this mascot.

been to many dinosaur museums, and this one is organized very well. Each room showcases creatures from a different era. We take many photos, including the requisite pose of being chased by a Velociraptor. Kristy purchases her obligatory souvenir from the gift shop—a little Triceratops—that becomes our mascot on the dashboard.

We have a fascination with dinosaurs.

We say goodbye to the old bones, get back on the road, and try to remember the Seven New Wonders of the World. I think passing time in a car spurs unique challenges and random trivia.

The temptation to use Google sets in. The struggle is real. We guess the Colosseum, Great Wall of China, Machu Picchu, and the Grand Canyon, knowing some are incorrect. It might even be the eight wonders! We don't know. After a while, we give up and enjoy the scenery.

Don't you go reaching for your phone to find the Seven Wonders! It's okay not to know. Go with the flow, and drive on with us. There can be life without the instant answers we are all so accustomed to Google providing us.

Some of our views could have been paintings.

Entering Page, Arizona

We drive through Monument Valley and cross into Arizona, nearing Page. We have a good friend named Paige, so we decide to stop by the, Entering Page sign and take a photo. There's no limit to where we will stop for a silly photo.

We haven't lost our 8th grade sense of humor.

Kristy holds up her fist—thumb side down—and pokes her other index finger in the hole, symbolizing sexual intercourse (literally, entering Paige). It's nice to have time for these fine moments.

We see signs for Antelope Canyon tours and stop to chat and book a tour. I'd been through the canyons twenty years ago, but I'm excited to return and see what Kristy might capture through the Nikon lens. The tour folks are friendly and accommodating and recommend a hike called Horseshoe Bend.

We take the hike and are mesmerized by the view. It is an overlook of the Colorado River flowing through the canyon, a thousand feet below. Looking over the edge makes us dizzy. It's a long way down! We spend sunset at the Horseshoe Bend overlook.

Obligatory couples shot at Horseshoe Bend

There is a local rumor that a guy pushed his wife off the edge, she grabbed him last minute, and they both fell. She landed twenty feet below, but as for him... I guess the gal felt what's good for the goose is good for the gander!

Night is approaching. We pass a few campgrounds; they're full. We decide to find a hotel, get out of the car, and explore the town. We're increasingly aware of how much money and frustration smart technology would save us right now as we stop at hotel after hotel, park, run in to ask the price, and drive on to the next. Drive in, drive out. Drive in, drive out.

Once we reach our limit of running around, we decide to settle on the next hotel we see, whatever the cost. It isn't the cheapest, but I am done for the day! Our hotel is a block away from a bowling alley. The rest of the night will be a blur. Going old school and enduring the frustration has directed us straight into a great evening.

- Bar-hopping
- Bowling alley
- "Steerike!
- Another strike!"
- Meet Parky the bartender
- Singing; Dancing
- Getting the locals all wound up

Everything is fair game while bar-hopping.

Day Two Thoughts

We're only two days into our journey, and I'm feeling both the strong pull of technology and the rewards of ignoring its call. There's an incredible sense of freedom when the digital leash comes off. Hunting for a hotel without apps at the end of a long day was no fun. (In all fairness, hunting for a hotel online at the end of a long day isn't much fun either.) On the other hand, ending up walking distance from a raucous bowling alley by pure chance gives the whole evening a little more magic.

It's hard to believe smartphones have only been around ten years or so. My phone feels like another part of me that's always been there. Over the past couple of days I've caught myself reaching in my pocket to grab my phone and check on friends, news, gossip, weather, the latest funny video, or anything that feels like it's connecting me to the rest of the world. The question is: are these connections real, and are they important? All I know is I find it hard not to look. Once the addiction gets you, it's hard to shake it. It reminds me of a story I often tell in the bar.

When I was a child, a dirt road at the end of our paved street led to the back bays of southern coastal New Jersey and the Seaview Docks— there for fishing, crabbing, and boat-launching. I was there, my bike piled among scores of other children's, every day of every summer.

Some locals nicknamed me Crab Trap John because I was so fond of catching blue crabs. I

My childhood sanctuary, Seaview Docks, Linwood, NJ.

liked using the handline method in addition to the traditional crab trap. I tied bait to the end of a long weighted string, threw it in the water, and waited for a crab to take it. When I felt the nibble, I pulled the line in at a painstakingly slow pace. The crab is so focused on eating it won't let go of the bait; it doesn't realize it's being led to its demise in human hands and then a pot of hot water.

TIP / It is important to pull the phone away ever so slightly so as not to arouse suspicion from your prey.

"Here's an experiment you can try," I tell whoever happens to be listening to my story. Slowly, very slowly, try to take away someone's phone while he is texting. He will follow the phone with both hands, still typing away. You can lead him in any direction as long as you pull it slowly, much like the crab on the string, but he won't let go of the phone. How far can a human be led? Could we be led to a pot of hot water, and from there, to our demise?

My listeners laugh, and we talk more. It's funny, and not, at the same time. We all know we're willing participants in a kind of a mind-robbing addiction. Remember those games people played on their phones, running around town looking for invisible characters? Some people walked right into traffic! In the blockbuster movie, WALL·E, there's a scary part of the plot where humans relied so much on technology and automation that they lost their ability to walk.

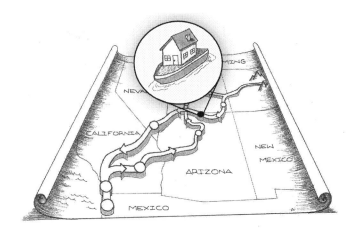

Day Three
Navajo Smoke Song: A Prayer

"Two roads diverged in a wood, and I—I took
the one less traveled by, And that has made all
the difference."

—Robert Frost,
"The Road Not Taken"

May 3, 2017
Destination: Las Vegas, Nevada

Bright and early and hungover!

Still no relapse into the social media world.
All our experiences are personal, and we are still
smiling and looking for the next humans with
whom to interact.

After a carb-loaded breakfast of leftovers to counter our queasiness, we're off to the tour of Antelope Canyon we booked yesterday with Antelope Canyon X.

We meet our guide—a local Navajo Indian named Tilman—and jump into the company SUV with four French folks and another couple from the Evergreen, Colorado, area. Then, we head to the canyons.

Our best tour guide ever, Tilman takes time to adjust every camera and phone to filter in proper lighting as we enter the canyon. Yes, I pull my phone out—but just for the camera. I swear I just used the camera!

Tilman recounts a bit of cool history and tells us some Navajo stories, then disappears into the canyon ahead. We suddenly hear a Native American flute resonating beautiful music through the canyon. When he returns, Tilman shares details of Navajo traditional ceremonies. He explains their use of peyote as medicine, and the guy from Evergreen says, "I remember my first time eating peyote caps!" We all giggle at this, including Tilman.

The natural light beaming through the canyon creates gorgeous shadows and highlights that inspire us all; soon, each of us is busily clicking away, attempting to capture the beauty around us. Tilman then asks us to stand in a circle while he sings the smoke song, which is a prayer. He asks us not to record this song but just to listen. This feels like a powerful sign that we are aligned on this trip.

His voice fills the canyon; the emotions we feel together are powerful. I am moved to tears,

Nature's canvas in Antelope Canyon, Page, AZ.

and I feel so lucky to be experiencing this once-in-a-lifetime moment. I'm in awe of the depth of connection available to all of us. I truly hope the flat screen won't prevent eager minds from experiencing such magic in the future. Will our generation, and future generations, remember to look up and reach out?

Along with his cash tip, I sign and give Tilman a copy of my book, Weedgalized in Colorado: True Tales from the High Country. He smiles, and we say our goodbyes. Tilman stays behind to wait for the next group while the rest of us hike out of the canyon. As I turn to look back at him one last time, I see he is now sitting on a rock, reading my book. I can't say exactly why I find this so touching, but I do.

As we hike back, I wonder: would we even have noticed the roadside sign for Antelope Canyon tours if we hadn't been app-free? I'm feeling very grateful.

We reach our car and drive next to the visitor center, adjacent to the Glen Canyon Dam. This dam is an amazing example of hard work and persistence. The visitor center displays old photos of how

Our best guide ever, Tilman. Thank you.

the dam was built, rerouting the river to complete the process.

Bridge over Glen Canyon, AZ.

Next, we fuel up, pass the always-beautiful Lake Powell, and head to Las Vegas for our Cirque du Soliel show.

We decide to lessen our time on the road and use our paper map to find back roads for shortcuts. We locate one taking us near Zion National Park. We have no idea if we'll be able to go around the park or will have to drive through it, and we won't know until we reach the park's gate.

When we get there, we learn that not only do we have to go through Zion National Park; we also have to pay the thirty-dollar entry fee. There is no turning back at this point or we'll miss our show. This is what happens when you don't have

access to smart technology. Damn, thirty bucks!
Oh well, might as well enjoy Zion and capture some
cool photos. We just don't yet know how lucky our
unexpected detour will prove to be!

Kristy and Johnny's 5 Fun Facts

1. Zion's name is credited to Mormon pioneer
   Isaac Behunin, who believed it to be a place of
   refuge from religious persecution.
2. Brigham Young later visited and found tobacco
   and wine being used and declared it "not Zion."
3. Within Zion's 229-square mile park are
   spectacular cliffs, canyons, and wilderness full
   of the unexpected.
4. Zion National Park is home to Kolob Arch, one
   of the world's largest arches, spanning 310
   feet.
5. Originally proclaimed as Mukuntuweap
   National Monument in 1909, it was established
   as Zion National Park in 1919.

The views in Zion National Park don't disappoint.

We laugh while complaining about how our poor road choices have cost us thirty bucks until Kristy notices the fine print on the receipt. If we save it and visit another national park within one week, we can put the original amount toward an eighty-dollar annual pass that's valid at all national parks. We abruptly stop complaining. We can make our road trip even more stellar!

We refer to the paper map and weigh our options, finding dozens of national parks within reach of our road trip. Discovering places to go on a paper map seems both much easier and more exciting than any online map search I've done. Maybe it's something about the way the brain interacts with the paper—or simply the size of the map. Size does matter!

We begin planning a whole new route for the way home that will lead us back through Zion, Joshua Tree, the Grand Canyon, and Bryce National Parks.

Serendipity.

Spontaneity.

Slow down and live.

Yes to all of that. We will find a way to visit another national park and purchase an annual pass within the next week. I've always loved the path less traveled.

Leaving Arizona

Our path from Arizona to Las Vegas using our paper map has us cutting it close. We arrive in

Las Vegas last minute, check into Harrah's, lug the longboard up through the casino and throw it above the TV, get changed, and taxi to Cirque du Soleil's KÀ.

After the show, we taxi back to Harrah's, go to the Flamingo Casino, and play video poker.

An amped guy at the bar gives us ten bucks, explaining that the casino was going to take it anyway. We head to Harrah's piano bar—hot girls on Dueling Pianos— and party way too late, leaving each of the gals with a copy of my book before retiring for the night.

Viva Las Vegas!

Feeling the levity of a digital detox road trip.

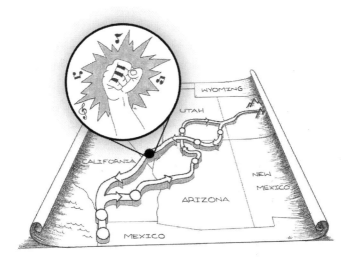

Day Four
You Changed My Perspective

"In the realm of ideas everything depends
on enthusiasm."
—Johann Wolfgang von Goethe

May 4, 2017
Location: Still Vegas

We wake up a little groggy—Vegas has that
effect on people. We decide to throw on our
swimsuits and cover-ups (a tank top for me,
something a little nicer for Kristy) and take a
quick swim before breakfast at noon. On our
way to the pool, we see the casino and can't
resist. I the hear bells and whistles and my
ADD kicks into high gear.

I run off, ending up at a video poker game at the bar. It takes Kristy a good fifteen minutes to find me; I'm already on drink number two, and we still haven't had breakfast. We make our way to the pool.

We pause at something shiny for a photo.

The lifeguard/bouncer won't let us in with outside drinks. I tell him it's just water, and he laughs; he's heard it before. Then I suggest, "They're not technically from outside since they're from inside at Harrah's casino floor, and isn't this Harrah's pool?"

"Yes, and nice try," he says, not buying that one either. We shrug it off and tell him we'll be back later. He smiles.

We venture back to the casino and decide food is a good idea. (If I ever write Johnny's Guide: Things to Do in Las Vegas, it would be the shortest book ever published, with just one instruction: "Wander around and do what looks interesting." It's a system for a great time that has yet to fail me.)

We end up at Guy Fieri's restaurant next door to the casino, and they won't let us in with a drink either; so, we sit outside, slam our drinks, and enter legally and eagerly.

There is a waiting list for a table for two. We prefer to sit at the bar and chat with the bartenders anyway, so we belly up to the almost-full bar and sit in the middle. Kristy's beautiful rainbow-colored dreadlocks attract a lot of attention. People often gravitate toward us and want to know our story; this bar is no different.

Soon after we have beers in front of us, two gentlemen across the bar—Michael and Bello— compliment Kristy's unique hair. They are very friendly, and both have magnificent smiles. They ask where we hail from and what we are up to in Sin City. We begin to tell them about our road trip, speaking loudly across the bar, and the servers and bartenders glance over in our direction, listening.

"Yeah, it's a crazy and fun idea. Our smartphones are turned off, and we're relying on paper maps to navigate five states and one foreign country. It's a break from smart technology, mainly social media. We're only allowed to text our mothers every few days and check my business email once in the morning."

One of the bartenders walks over and puts her elbows on the bar. She has a dazed look in her eye. She almost chokes, "You're doing what?" She introduces herself as Laura, and wants to know all about it.

"How is it going so far? I would love to do something like that. Kudos to you both. What a great idea! That is awesome!" rapid fire from Laura.

Britteny, another bartender, hears Laura and asks, "What's she talking about? What are you guys up to?"

I feel like we're on a journey to find a buried treasure. There is curiosity from every direction—a buzz in the air. Excitement! People crowd in around us, asking for details. Michael is now standing behind us, peppering us with questions. We're a little embarrassed, aware that our crazy social experiment was possibly more of a whim than a major commitment; but we're a little proud, too.

Michael, Bello, and Britteny want to hang out with us later that evening and we make plans to meet. We exchange numbers (we write theirs on paper napkins, calculating that, if we have to text or call them as a last resort, we can fit contacting them into our 95% unplugged requirement). I have a couple of books on me as always—this time I've put them in a plastic bag to take to the pool—and I shamelessly put a few copies out on the bar for all to see. I end up gifting a copy each to Michael and Britteny. They are stoked to have a book signed from an author at a bar.

The day bartender, Laura, is finishing up her shift and says goodbye to us. I watch her leave. I am not attracted to her, although she is beautiful; but she still draws my attention. She reaches the doorway—one arm in her jacket and the other still grasping for the other sleeve—turns around, and walks back over to us at the bar.

"I have to tell you guys, you really had an impact on my point of view. You changed my perspective today, and I wanted to thank you."

Goosebumps. We didn't expect our experiment to have any kind of impact on other people; neither of us realized our fun idea could actually touch and inspire others. How crazy that only a decade after they debuted on the popular market a sixteen-day break from smartphones is seen as so meaningful! More light bulbs: I'm thinking big again. Maybe one day, this book will move millions of people to slow down, unplug and enjoy each other more!

The rest of the afternoon, we play in the pool (finally), gamble, shower, and dress up.

We're excited; it's early evening and time to go see esteemed and funny author, David Sedaris. We bought our tickets two months ago, and now we're headed to the Smith Center for Performing Arts. Showtime is 7:30 p.m., but we've arrived early, as I like to do. Can you believe there is a bar in the lobby? Shocking, right?

While we're in line for cocktails, a woman compliments Kristy's hair, and we strike up a conversation. She tells us we can buy one of David's books at the merchandise table, just twenty feet away, and ask him to sign it. We look over. He's sitting at a desk with a line of eager fans queuing up to get his autograph.

It doesn't take long for me to select my next David Sedaris book and hop into his autograph line. Squirrel Seeks Chipmunk: A Modest Bestiary seems like a great choice. (This book will soon come into play in other ways on our unplugged journey. Stay tuned!)

It is getting close to showtime. The usher keeps looking at her watch and gauging how long the line is, to determine whether the author will have enough time for everyone before he must prepare for his show. She walks over to me, and I half expect her to say, "Sorry, but he won't have enough time for you."

Instead, she tells me I will be the last one to see him before the show. He does sign books after the show as well, but I am in go-mode and happy to be the last in line.

"Hello David, I'm Johnny, and this is my girlfriend, Kristy."

He is so friendly and seems genuinely pleased to meet us. I quickly tell him how his writing, style, and delivery have influenced me. I tell him about my book and thank him for inspiring me. With much respect and all my manners, I ask if he would like a copy.

"I know you must get a lot of gifts, and I don't want to burden you with another. But...I happen to have a couple of copies on me, and if you would like one, I'd be honored," I say.

"I'd love a copy, but you have to sign it for me."

I can't believe it. One of my favorite authors is asking me to sign my book for him! I hope he can read what I signed because I'm trembling a little bit from the thrill.

Kristy and I have spectacular seats in the upper-box section just above the stage. We love

David Sedaris writes me a personal note.

the show. If David Sedaris ever comes to a town near you, go see him. There's nothing like an evening with him. His stories are poignant and hilarious and different from any other kind of entertainment. We feel connected to him at some deep level, although superficially we're so different. He seems to have that effect on everyone in the audience. Thank you again, David, for this moment.

Our second day in Vegas is far from over. After the Sedaris show, we:

- explore and people-watch on Fremont street
- watch other tourists zip-lining down the middle of the street
- try to meet Britteny the bartender where we said we'd meet, but are unable find her in the massive crowds

39

- find Michael from the bar
- see street shows galore with street performers every hundred feet
- almost get run over by a guy dressed as a centaur in a thong dancing
- stop and listen to amazing street rappers—we agree they deserve a recording contract!
- are accosted by a woman in a sexy devil costume who just has to tell us how much she loves Kristy's look
- return to Harrah's piano bar and sing and dance until

...drunk and tired, we are ready for bed and make our way into the elevator. As the doors close, a gentleman jumps on. We watch and feel his anxiety. He seems uncomfortable and fumbles for something to pass the awkward time.

I watch him grab his smartphone. He holds it down by his waist, his thumb hovering over several different apps. He doesn't know which one to choose. I immediately think of a new word to describe what I am seeing: "thover- the act of a human thumb hovering over a screen as the human mindlessly tries to decide which button to push."

He doesn't seem to have a reason to look at anything as his thumb wanders aimlessly over his smartphone screen. It's like a knee-jerk reaction to grab the phone and then make a BIG life decision. Which app do I choose? Which app do I choose? Which app do I choose?

Frightening New Terminology

Maybe my new term will stick. New words are popping into our vocabulary all the time to describe our interactions with technology. Nomophobia (no-mobile phobia), for example, is defined as the fear of not having your smartphone on you. Some argue it's a type of an anxiety disorder, and, for some people, I guess it is must be a very real fear.

Thumb zombies are on the rise. Smartphone overuse is becoming so rampant there are smartphone addiction centers popping up all over the world. In Germany, people's smartphone habits have become so dangerous a company has put lights in the ground to minimize pedestrian-involved traffic accidents; and, in China, city authorities are experimenting with sidewalk lanes for cell phone users.

There's also a new word that describes when couples hang out together but ignore each other, focusing instead on smartphone surfing: phubbing.

Phubbing

the practice of ignoring one's companion or companions in order to pay attention to one's phone or other mobile device. (See phubbing in appendix for more info. I cannot believe there is an anti-phubbing movement and it's pretty thorough.)

---

[1] For information on what you can do to raise awareness of and stop phubbing, see Twisted Topics #4.

Distraction Technologies
a term given to the devices of today that may be guilty of stealing our attention spans. Examples include, but are not limited to: smartphones, tablets, iPads, mobile devices, etc.

Digital Dementia
a phrase first used by German neuroscientist named Manfred Spitzer in his book of the same name. He defines it as the overuse of technology resulting in a reduction of our cognitive abilities that is seen in patients with head and brain trauma or psychiatric illness.

Hello Facebook world, I'm looking for some fun interaction here.
What are some names, phrases, and/or terms that have been created in the last ten years since the advent of smartphones and social media?
Here are some examples; tweeting, updating your status, Facebooking, sexting, phubbing, nomophobia, etc. (comment below) I'm working on a chapter in my upcoming book and would love some input, especially from social media.
Have fun and thank you!!
Coming soon: A vote for favorite title of this upcoming book!!!

How did we ever get by for thousands of years without smartphones, and how did they become so essential to us in such a short time?

When we return from our trip, I decide to use social media to talk to friends about the language of social media.

Responses came in a twenty-four hour period:

Matt: Bluetooth douche

Crystal: Facebook Official

Karla: I think a lot of these things become "verbs" in and of them self like you mentioned facebooking, tweeting, etc. The other day I told someone I "venmo'd" them! Also (this isn't quite what you're asking for) but the social (media) norm to make life events "Facebook official"

Kimmie: Click bait

Crystal: Hashtag anything

Matt: Ping me

Blair: Dear autocorrect, by now you should know I never mean to type 'duck' Also, we're too lazy to spell anymore...tbh, np, ty, btw, omg, smh, wth, wtf, stfu...you get the idea

John: Instabrag

Corey: Troll

Alan: Drunk dial/text, butt dial, blocked, share, steal, pirate or thepiratebay. Realtime loc, chillaxin, rasterbator, spam, warez ohnosecond

Randi: FaceTime, videogram, screenshot, PM, Insta, Instafamous, Scrolling your newsfeed

Matt: Is "ghost" one?

Jaremy: catfished

Hannah: Selfie

Tom: Ponzi

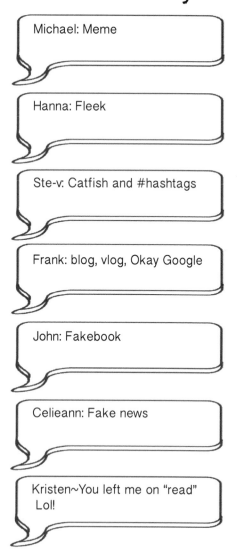

Michael: Meme

Hanna: Fleek

Ste-v: Catfish and #hashtags

Frank: blog, vlog, Okay Google

John: Fakebook

Celieann: Fake news

Kristen~You left me on "read" Lol!

Jeremy: TLDNR - Too Long Did Not Read

Austin: Crackberry, those always smashed blackberry phones

Misty: "CAN YOU HIT ME BACK" I love this one. I'm always reluctant to text this lol

Misty: I think the Urban Dictionary is an absolute must.

Simone: Ghosting

Valerie: PM me

Heidi: 'Trolling- aka ppl looking through newsfeeds to argue...hah!

Marj: This is an epic thread!

Lauri: BUMP

Joy: LOL, OMG, hashtag, Bitmoji, unfriend, clumsy thumbsy, swipe right, "damn you autocorrect!", Google it

Nick: Finstagram

Mike: butt dial, swipe right, unlike

Stephanie: Phishing, IM or message me, going viral

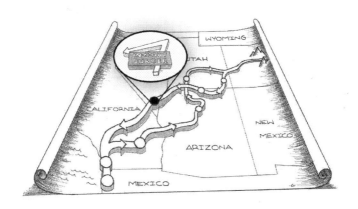

Day Five
When the Heck is Cinco de Mayo?

"I'll bet you twenty bucks I can get you gambling
before the end of the day."

—Lloyd Christmas,
Dumb and Dumber, 1994

May 5, 2017
Location: Still Vegas

We decide to extend our stay in Vegas for one more
night of debauchery. It's Cinco de Mayo, after all.

We start our day at our new favorite restaurant,
Guy Fieri's Vegas Kitchen. We hope to see familiar
faces, and we aren't disappointed. Britteny is
behind the bar and greets us with her beautiful
smile. We recount endless tales from the night

before. I joke about inventing T-shirts next year for Cinco de Mayo that say something like, "When the heck is Cinco de Mayo?" Get it? Cinco means five and Mayo means May, so the name and date of the holiday are exactly the same. It's okay. I'm the only one laughing in the restaurant, too. I tend to make myself—and nobody else—laugh quite often.

We go back to our room for my daily business email check, and I find out about an errand I have to run for my book promotion. Luckily, I accidentally read an email from my friend Paul that is mixed in with my business emails. Paul lives in Vegas—I think—and I had emailed him before we left to tell him about our trip.

What I don't know until I read the email is he doesn't live in Vegas; he and his wife, Christina, live in LA but are visiting Vegas right now and staying just down the road, next door to our new favorite restaurant! I email him back right away, and we follow up by text to arrange to meet for lunch. (Yes, reading the email is borderline against road trip rules, and I probably shouldn't write him back and definitely shouldn't text. We get over it, guilt-free, knowing we are still below five percent usage; and, really, if the universe hits you over the head with synchronicity like this, you gotta listen!)

Paul and I worked together at a pub in Dillon, Colorado, years ago. He was the head bouncer, and I was a bartender. We were young and carefree; in other words, if I ever tell the stories of the trouble we got into at that bar, I'll have to change all the names.

Paper Maps, No Apps

We decide to meet Paul and Christina at Margaritaville, just a few steps away from our hotel. They are seated at the bar when we arrive, and my back is well-adjusted after one of Paul's patented bear hugs. They want to know all about Kristy: how long we have been together, how we met, and where are we heading. We love telling our story and jump right in, taking turns narrating.

This trip marked our first full year together. We met two years ago at the Smok N' Bra boutique in Frisco, Colorado. Kristy was working behind the counter, and I was at the store to interview its owner for Weedgalized in Colorado: True Tales from the High Country. The shop sells smoking devices, art, jewelry, bras and other lingerie, and, shall we say, romance enhancers. It's a really cool place, and I stopped in from time to time. Maybe at first I was interested in the merchandise, but I became increasingly more interested in the saleswoman. It took me a few months, but I finally worked up the courage to ask her out, and she said, "No." Actually, I heard, "No." She didn't really say anything. I took the silence as a no and gracefully departed.

I ran into her at a local watering hole a week later, spying her at the bar and sitting next to her. She said she was taken aback when I asked her out. She couldn't believe the locally famous bartender was interested. That was the reason for the nonresponse, but I had taken her silence as rejection. Boy, am I glad I saw her this day!

I believe I've established I like corny jokes. In fact, I love the ridiculous. I always keep a few jokes, gags, and tricks in my pockets. Most of the time, I will have fake spiders, snakes, false teeth, and plastic tongues. On that fateful day, when I ran into Kristy, I was carrying a big fake dog poop. I pulled the big fake poop out of my pocket, put it on the bar and asked, "Can you believe this shit?" Cynical people might—and do—roll their eyes at a goofball stunt like that. Kristy didn't, though. She laughed uncontrollably, and we've laughed and joked together ever since. My fake poop was the catalyst to winning her over, and we love the shit out of each other! We fell head over heels, and the rest is history.

Reliving our story with Paul and Christina puts us all in the mood to get silly, Las Vegas style. Shots! We agree this will be a great idea, but there is that errand to run for my book promo. I have to mail a package.

Whew! Work, work, work. Paul used to live in Las Vegas and knows where to find a UPS store. He and I leave the women, now chatting away like old friends. This allows us to speak candidly about the gals and vice versa. We all enjoy the inside scoop, don't we?

We're back in fifteen minutes, ready to find some trouble on the Strip in the hot sun. We tell ourselves we deserve a day out on the town after all the postal work we just did, and we're easily convinced.

We happen on a courtyard in front of Caesars Palace, filled with about a dozen games of cornhole. You can, if you like, bet drinks on the outcome—and we do. There is a daiquiri bar on site. This will be our home for the next few hours. Throwing bean bags, singing, dancing, laughing, drinking, and taking photos fill our day with good cheer.

Paul and Christina have tickets to a show tonight, and we need to eat to slow down the insanity, so we say our reluctant goodbyes and go our separate ways.

The Bet

It seems every time I travel, no matter how remote the destination, I run into someone I know. I usually make a betting game out of this when my traveling companions are willing. There's just one rule: everyone on the vacation puts five dollars in the pot. The first person to see someone he knows wins the pot. You just can't arrange the meeting in advance. It has to be unexpected.

 TIP Rules for The Bet: At the beginning of a trip or a vacation, all that want to participate must agree to these rules. The first person to see a friend or acquaintance will receive $5 from all the other travelers in the group. It must be random, not prearranged.

I won the bet our first day in Vegas. On Fremont Street, when we were taking in all the sights and sounds at about the same pace as our drinks, a group of four people yelled out my name. They remembered I was their bartender on a trip to Frisco. Crazy! They looked familiar, but I couldn't recall their names. Most times, I only know first names and the drink of choice anyway. They knew who I was, though, and where I worked. Kristy had to agree they were acquaintances, and that was enough to win the pot. Hooray, five bucks!

Today, I hit the Vegas jackpot. We find an In & Out Burger. This chain hasn't reached Colorado yet, so eating there is a tradition for me. We have a healthy dinner of burgers and fries and walk down a side street where we randomly bump into my friend, known as Big Jon, and his groomsmen. We had RSVP'd to Jon and Rebecca's wedding invitation just before we left home and now, here is the groom in the flesh. I win five bucks again!

Big Jon is aptly nicknamed. He's big:— muscular, not rotund—and he's originally from New Jersey but now lives a town over from us in Colorado. His eight buddies are all from New Jersey, and needless to say, we all hit it off pretty well. Jersey jokes are flying as we join forces and partake in our favorite activity in Vegas: gallivanting. With drinks in hand and dance moves lifting our feet, we sashay our way up and down the Strip, stopping in stores to refill drinks and in casinos to test our luck.

As the night goes on and the memories begin to turn foggy, we run into Paul and Christina again on the casino floor. I say hello and run and hide because of an embarrassing case of the hiccups. That is the last time I see them on this trip. Damn hiccups.

I have never played craps, but Big Jon teaches me as the commotion around the table reels me in. Between hiccups, I place my bets, and, within minutes, I win almost a hundred dollars. Somehow, my autopilot goes into high intellect mode. I grab my winnings and Kristy, say our goodbyes, and retreat to our room. This is our earliest night in bed: 1:00 a.m.

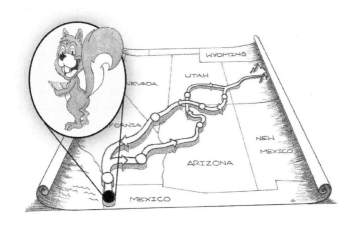

Day Six
Peggy Sue

"Everybody gets so much information all day long
that they lose their common sense."
—Gertrude Stein,
"Reflection on the Atomic Bomb"

May 6, 2017
Destination: Rosarito, Mexico

Several cups of coffee downed? Check.

Fast food with french fries, extra salty to help
with the hangovers, consumed? Check.

Sunglasses on? Check.

We're ready to check our paper map and hit
the highway. We leave Vegas and soon enter
California, one of our favorite states to visit. A

new day and a new state: adventures await.

We're on our way to a private beachside bungalow in Rosarito, Mexico, a resort town just ten or so miles south of the US border, not too far from Tijuana. We had booked the private residence a few months before through Airbnb.

We begin seeing signs for Peggy Sue's 50's Diner right after crossing the state line even though it's in Yermo, California, a couple of hours ahead of us. The closer we get, the more signs we see; this makes us curious and hungry, one

Kristy gets very excited at border crossings.

heck of a combination. We feel so light without schedules or the call of technology weighing

Vintage cars in front of Peggy Sue's Diner.

us down. We pull into the diner's parking lot. Complete with classic cars parked out front, this attraction does not disappoint.

Kristy has an affinity for all things vintage, so she is now in her glory. Memorabilia is organized into sections, by decades or by topic, in several different rooms. The fifties dominate, but there's also Betty Boop, Wizard of Oz, Finding Nemo, kitty cat clocks with ticking tails, Snoopy, and Gumby— not to mention an old-fashioned soda fountain, a replica of a five and dime counter, and an ice cream parlor.

We enjoy it all. We sit. We eat. We shop. We set back out on our journey. Thank you, Peggy Sue!

I love finding little gems like this; it's what road trips are all about.

Our next stop is San Diego, to visit an old friend from New Jersey. Matt da Ritt was a badass surfer in New Jersey, and he still rips when it comes to the waves. A good friend and solid character, he is one to count on. He used to live in Rosarito, and he gives us useful tips about how to get there and about roads in Mexico.

Driving across the border in the pre-wall era.

We convince him to join us in Mexico tomorrow. Our time with him in San Diego is short as we want to get to our bungalow before dark, so we take a quick tour of his house, finalize our plans for tomorrow, and once again get on our way.

Despite our efforts to arrive in daylight, evening is already upon us and night is fast approaching. We soon realize we'll have to employ the undeniable benefits of technology on this part of the journey. A wrong turn could land us in Tijuana. It's a fun town to visit, but I don't want to drive my new car, full of our valuables, there at night. Mexico is a beautiful country and I'm sure it is safe in many places, but I've been warned. I don't want to get lost there. We turn on GPS.

Paper Maps, No Apps

Almost immediately after we cross the border, we notice Mexican roads are very different from those in the US. They're darker, and the road paint dividing traffic lanes is hard to see; there are so many potholes we have to slow down considerably; and, the number of drivers on the road seems to have tripled.

Boom. Pothole. Beep beep!

We make it to Rosarito, turn off GPS, and use the Airbnb directions we printed to try to find the tiny trail that leads to our bungalow.

It's now fully dark. Our printed directions say the turnoff is just ahead, but I don't know what that means. It feels like distances are different here, or maybe it's just that we've lost the ability to gauge distance without GPS. But, then again, even before I started using GPS, I was curious about how we experience distance. What I mean is this: when told your turn is just a few meters ahead or just a few minutes away and you can't miss it, you will surely miss it. How does that happen?

It's all part of the fun of travel, especially when you're off the app and in the moment. Not only are you forced sometimes to puzzle through obscure directions and distances, it makes most of us get philosophical: where do things really exist in this space-time continuum?

Over a river (we drive through a large puddle) and through the woods (we notice tall marine reeds waving in the dark on the sides of the road), we arrive at our bungalow on the beach. From what we can see in the dark—and confirm the next day—it is just as promised. Beautiful, bright colors and a touch of adobe greet us. The owners left us a welcome note on the front porch, held down under a tall and skinny bottle of Don Ramón tequila. "Shots? Sure! Why not? If you insist!" I exclaim excitedly to Kristy, picking up the liquor.

We bring the Don Ramón and our stuff into the bungalow, and, like kids, run through our home away from home with cameras in hand, snapping photos of the unique architecture and cool colors.

The house has only one floor, but we find a staircase outside to a rooftop deck that overlooks the beach and ocean, which we can hear and even see a bit in the dark. We can't wait to see what this looks like in the morning.

We spend some time toasting the beautiful location and the bungalow. The temperature drops, and it begins to rain; so, we retreat into the bungalow, close the windows, and prepare the wood-burning chiminea-shaped fireplace for the cozy fire we plan to light later in the evening.

The rain has turned into a downpour, but we don't care. We decide to take a walk in search of fun and food. We manage to find our way onto a path to the town's main road, which we walk down for just five minutes before stumbling upon an Italian restaurant. The sign out front reads "Betuccini's Pizzeria & Trattoria," but they don't look open. It's dark all around the restaurant. We peer into the windows, but we can't see much of anything. We cautiously try the front door, and it opens. It's so dark inside we feel, for a moment, a little scared. The entryway resembles a cave with low clearance. Then, the smells of garlic and simmering sauces hit us, and we know we're where we're meant to be. The dim hall opens into a beautiful restaurant with a warm feel. We've discovered a wonderful secret—and all off-line.

When we sit down, I notice my first instinct is still to take out my phone and surf my apps while waiting for the server. No dice on this trip: Kristy and I must sit and look at each other and at the restaurant's decor. We have to talk to each other. How weird!

When I think about how I might describe the feeling to someone younger, I hear myself saying, "Back in the day, we sat and looked at each other, and we talked." Back in the day. For most people, when we talked to each other in restaurants means just ten or fifteen years ago—before smartphones. But those were drastically different times.

 Pretend it's 1995 and talk to each other. (taken from a chalk board sign inside a coffee shop, Inxpot, in Keystone, Colorado. "*We don't have WIFI,,,,Pretend it's 1995 and talk to each other.*"

Sitting in Betuccini's with Kristy feels like playing an old board game that hasn't been brought out for a while. We observe and discuss the artwork and the creativity it took to choose where to display each painting. I'm enjoying the conversation and the fact we're noticing things we might otherwise ignore. With a smartphone to occupy the senses, who looks at decor?

Kristy notices some Italian words and phrases around the restaurant and asks me to translate. We are together: connecting and interacting. It is relaxing, and time feels like it's standing still. Living in the moment is unrehearsed poetry. The romance is overflowing at our table, lit by candles rather than electronic blue lights. We are present.

After what turns out to be an amazingly delicious meal, we run back through the rainstorm to the bungalow, dodging puddles and laughing. We have no problem finding it anymore; what was hidden to us just a few hours ago is now easy to find. I love how that happens!

From what we can see—the restaurant wasn't crowded, and there aren't many cars in front of the bungalows around ours—the little beach community where our rented bungalow sits is pretty vacant. I guess it isn't a peak time for tourism. We're okay with that. There isn't much close by as far as evening/nighttime activities either. With the rain coming down so hard, a nighttime walk on the beach is not very appealing. What to do? What to do? Until now, our nights have been full of adventures into the wee hours; suddenly, we're on our own.

We take a closer look around the bungalow. We have tequila from our hosts, beer from our cooler, games on the living room shelves. There is a wooden top with a string and mechanism to spin, nicely painted with brilliant colors and patterns. How does this contraption work? What is the best way to wind the string so it can be pulled out easily to spin the top? This is tonight's to-do list. A short list; we master it after a few tries.

Next to the top, painted in the same style, are two wooden cups, each with a handle on the bottom and a ball attached by a string to the handle. This one we get right away: hold the handle with the ball dangling below, and swing the ball up to catch in the cup. After a few attempts, we seem to be getting it. Okay, so now we have a potential activity, and we have refreshments.

We discover these antique games in our beach bungalow.

Next, we challenge ourselves to come up with a way to use the two toys in one game. That's easy. We take turns spinning the top on the floor, and, while it is spinning, count how many times we each can land our ball in our cup. We talk and play and count and laugh, too, at how easy it is to find alternative activities in a town with no nightlife, even without apps.

Being easily amused is a good thing.

Kristy has enough of me winning and is ready for the next big event. We resume our exploration of the bungalow, looking for more

games and/or treasures. I zone in on the book
I just bought in Las Vegas, Squirrel Seeks
Chipmunk: A Modest Bestiary.

"How about you sit on the floor next to the fire
and I'll read to you?"

I barely finish my sentence before she sits,
poking the fire and waiting. I've never read a book
aloud to anyone before, and I like the idea.

I'm a big fan of audio books, especially those
by David Sedaris. His over-the-top humor keeps
me laughing out loud through most of his stories.
When I listen in my car, his voice takes me back
to my childhood. When he reads and imitates
family members, it reminds me of how I grew up.
Sometimes I catch myself looking in the rearview
mirror, half-expecting to see my mother in the
back seat.

I'm Italian, and my neighborhood friends were
mostly Jewish or Italian. David Sedaris sounds like
we sounded as kids when we imitated our mothers
and fathers in their overprotective panic mode.

"What do you mean you didn't make a
reservation at the restaurant? Don't you know
David might starve half to death? Meshuggener!"
my friends would mock.

Or, regarding my own life, I may say, "Don't
forget to call your father on his birthday! You know
how he worries, and you'll give him the agita."

I wonder if my mother really believes he
will become ill if the phone doesn't ring, and I
wonder how birthday well-wishes are somehow
tied to my dad's digestive tract. I think my mom

probably does believe it. And yes, it is the agita, not just agita.

My mom is well trained in the panic arts, with a minor in worried phrases and demands. "Where were you? Why haven't you called? I almost called the police looking for you!"

It's funny how similar Italian and Jewish moms can be, at least in my experience.

I try my hand at reading to Kristy the way I think David would read it, complete with the inflections typical of our families. Kristy sits there, eyes focused on one spot on the wall. She looks like she's seeing the events I'm describing, so I pause to show her the book's sketches and illustrations. She smiles.

One of the stories involves a breakup between a squirrel and a chipmunk, and Kristy tears up at the end of this romance. This is how we pass our evening in a rainstorm in a bungalow on the beach in Mexico. The fire in the fireplace is the icing on the cake. About a third of the way through the book, something triggers us both; we begin talking at the same time, wondering together about life hundreds of years ago. We talk over each other and out of turn. We think we've discovered, or rediscovered, something important. A few more shots of tequila add to our conviction that we have significant advice to give the world, and we're ready to spread the news that we can save everyone from becoming zombies.

"Let's film our discussion on how we spent our evening and what has happened so far on our trip. We can share it later when we get back!" Kristy yells.

"How? On YouTube? It's an oxymoron! It's a paradox!" I holler back.

More beer washes down more tequila, and

> *Beach Bungalow Brainstorms*
> *A Play in Three Acts:*
> Act One: Tequila
> Act Two: Beer
> Act Three: Save the World
> Fin

the debate intensifies. How can we film ourselves while staying true to our social experiment? And, if we do film it, how can we promote it? We have to use social media to warn folks about the overconsumption of such platforms while engaging in those very platforms.

"Fuck it! We're doing it anyway," I say. "The best way to reach the folks and show them is to plant this secret message right in their own social media habits."

"Yeah, that's it," Kristy said. "We'll be imposters in that world in order to bring them back to their own fireplaces! Maybe they'll read this book by a fire!"

Not long after we return to app-world, we learn, along with everyone else, that Apple and others are now pushing apps to limit the use of apps. I found at least six apps that are designed to curtail app time. Some might call this new app category ironic. Others might call it hypocrisy and suspect it was generated more by PR departments than by a genuine concern about overuse. I guess I just call it reality, whatever the design motive. I mean, the kitchen timer or stopwatch would serve the same purpose, and I'm sure the new apps benefit the companies that produce them more than you and me; but, for now, I'd rather see people using the don't-overuse apps than not.

Watch the videos we made that night about our unplugged trip: www.johnnywelsh.com/videos

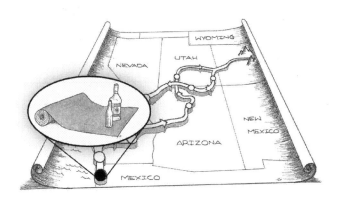

Day Seven
Tequila, Beer, and a Yoga Mat

"Every now and then go away, have a little relaxation, for when you come back to your work your judgement will be surer."

—Leonardo da Vinci

May 7, 2017
Location: Still Mexico

Today, we relax and catch up on organizing, journaling, and reading; then we do some driving and exploring to see the country. We head south along the beautiful Pacific coastline. I get a little nervous when I see the checkpoint with Mexican military soldiers standing in the road holding machine guns, observing cars going by and

Trying to look innocent while passing a military checkpoint.

stopping some. We are told to drive on through. I guess we don't look suspicious in Mexico.

We see a Walmart Supercenter from the highway and decide to make a supply run for more beer, tequila, and some Jameson Irish whiskey, all for creative writing purposes, of course.

Getting to Walmart turns out to be more arduous than we expect. The only way to turn left is from the passing lane on the highway, which means blocking all traffic in the lane behind me. I try not to panic, feeling all the while it's not a question of if, but when someone will rear-end us. A little old lady behind me, laying on the car horn for a hot minute, doesn't hesitate to let me know I should just go for it and charge oncoming traffic. I hold my breath and dart through the traffic only to find I'm in the middle of a maze of side roads. After plenty of wrong turns, we somehow achieve our quest: we have reached the Walmart parking lot.

Paper Maps, No Apps

A storm hits while we shop; the raindrops pound the roof so loudly we think there's a jet overhead. The sound drowns out the store music and intercom announcements. Oh no! I hope we don't miss any "azul-light specials" we heard before the storm began.

There are bargains everywhere. Kristy scores a super thick, high quality yoga mat. We shop for a good half hour, then stand in line with our bread, cheese, chocolates, Jameson, beer, tequila, and yoga mat. Imagine that on a hand-written shopping list!

The storm outside has ended, the clouds part, and we walk out into the fresh sunshine carrying the essentials for our Mexican beach bungalow vacation extravaganza.

"It's weird, but I'm in the mood for oysters for dinner," I say to Kristy.

"Not so weird," she says. "I am, too! But I'm pretty sure it's because we've passed the same giant billboard advertising oysters about ten times trying to find the Walmart."

She's right. I remember now. We get back on the highway, hunt for the oyster billboard, and soon see it (it's pretty hard to miss). "Blue Agua: The Best and Largest Oysters in Rosarito" it reads. We locate the restaurant, and pull in.

Turns out that, contrary to what you might assume, "Blue Agua" must be Spanish for "We are out of oysters," so we get tacos instead. We're now in downtown Rosarito and decide to stroll through the shops, stores, and charming mini-maze of an open market. My experiences with Kristy lead me to develop a theory: females love to shop after eating. Or, is it, before eating? I can't remember exactly.

We separate, each drawn to a different kind of souvenir. When I find Kristy, she is in a cute little old lady's booth. The lady looks about eighty and has wonderful smile, wrinkles around her mouth, and rainbow-arched lines on her forehead. Her face shows she has lived a long, happy life. Little do I know that before I showed up, she had produced a bottle of buyer's encouragement—tequila—and convinced Kristy to join her in two shots. Kristy ends up buying an expensive elephant bracelet, and I learn the real reason this shopkeeper has had a life full of many smiles.

Kristy and I visit a liquor store to purchase Swisher Sweets Little Cigars. A bottle of Don Ramón tequila beckons me; it's the same brand we learned to love just twelve hours ago. We buy that, too, and return to the bungalow to get dolled up for dinner.

On foot, we explore the main street near our bungalow, in search of food; and, zigzagging around deep puddles, we soon find Angus Bell, a steak house where we're served huge portions with frosty cervezas.

After dinner, we head to the little casino next door to kill time before meeting up with my Jersey friend, Matt da Ritt, at the bungalow. The casino is tiny—two or three rooms. Each person is required to fill out an information ticket with his passport credentials to obtain a white credit card-looking gambling card to load with pesos. It is an arcade for adults. We play. We break even.

We make our way back home, which is how we're starting to think of our bungalow, and head up to the roof to watch for Matt. He shows up a few minutes after we do and tells us he was just at Angus Bell ordering takeout. He told us he asked the staff if they had seen us, the "two gringos," as he described us. They sure had—just a few hours earlier! We all pile into Matt's car, head back to the steak house, and pick up his take out order.

"These are the two gringos I was looking for," Matt says in Spanish to the staff as we return. They all look at Matt and make the international sign for drinking—cupped hand in a sweeping motion from chest to mouth. They mean our drinking. Kristy and I had been enjoying ourselves rather noticeably at the old Angus Bell, I guess. Back to the bungalow!

- Fire in fireplace
- No music
- No electronics
- Matt and I reminisce about Mainland High, Holy Spirit, Ocean City, and Atlantic City high school friends, surf sessions, and parties
- Kristy pulls a Houdini and disappears to sleep

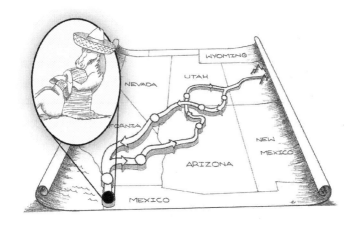

Day Eight
Poop River

"Other cultures live for today, while we
plan for tomorrow."

—Matt da Ritt

May 8, 2017
Location: Still Mexico

We all wake up with an unquenchable thirst,
chugging water while getting ready for Matt's local
tour. Matt drives us to an amazing place for tacos
and morning beers. It's a tradition in small coastal
Mexican towns that's arisen—I'm pretty sure—from
the need to feed Americans with hangovers.

The restaurant sign reads "Tapanco." Kristy
and I are surprised at the cool attractions inside

the restaurant and adjacent buildings. Everything is accessible from within the restaurant, over wooden walkways connecting them.

In the middle of the restaurant flows an eight-foot tall waterfall. We wander and see a lounge with tropical birds, cozy couches, and an old record player with an assortment of vinyl. Across a nearby walkway is a fresh bakery.

We find a table in the restaurant. The food and service are both off the charts, and we all feel like royalty as they keep our cups full. The frosted beer goblets feel like chalices. Our hangovers don't stand a chance. We sit tall in our chairs and sip with our pinkies out, laughing, reminiscing, and eating. We are feeling better by the minute.

Our first stop after Tapanco is a little fishing village. The drive down the dirt road to the water's edge is full of vendors enticing us to park near their booths as they show off their latest catch. Some hold up big crabs, and others display large fresh fish.

The hustle and bustle is alive and well. We are so happy to have a little local insight. I never would have known there was a hidden fishing village at the end of that dirt road. We decide to return for oysters later in the day.

It's time for sightseeing, and what do we choose to view first after our drunken night of steaks and storytelling? A giant Jesus, of course. Onward we press, on a pilgrimage to see the massive statue. We've heard the giant Jesus statue in Rio de Janeiro is even larger than the monolith we're on the way to see, so we decide to call it Jesús Hermano Pequeño, Jesus' little brother. It's our juvenile humor kicking in. We drive for a while, telling stories and laughing. And then...Jesus! There He is: arms open to the great Pacific Ocean. Doesn't He look taller than in all those paintings?

The next site on Matt's tour is not in any tour book. If you were to drive a car on this highway, you may even miss it, but Matt knows where to look. We stop at a convenience store for some road sodas, then head toward our destination: the Big Titty Woman.

Matt drives up to where this landmark is located and begins a complex series of maneuvers to park the car by the side of the road. He looks up to the left, then adjusts the angle of the car. He looks left again and adjusts

75 foot tall Christ of the Sacred Heart statue above the town of El Morro.

again. Clearly, the car has to be positioned exactly right for optimal viewing. We soon see why.

There it is, or, I should say, there they are—giant boobies on the side of a house, and above the boobies, a long neck and strange face. We second guess the Big Titty Woman. Is it, in fact, a woman? The face kind of looks like a man. Is it a man with tits? Or, is it a woman with no hair? The jaw line is very pronounced. We dissect the large construction from across the street in our car.

"Look at the collar bone and those shoulders. It is a man with tits!" one of us proclaims.

"Can't be, those tits are too nice."

"Yeah, that's the thing with fake tits, they're abnormally symmetrical."

Boobs on the Mexican coastline: the jokes continue. They're not very funny—I'll spare you—but, for us, it doesn't matter. We are laughing at anything at this point—total giggle mode.

We are allowing ourselves to be as immature as we want, and we're all accepting each other. Nobody is judging. Ah, life is good in these moments. We don't have a care in the world.

We chuckle even more at our juvenile humor and at the fact we are taking time out of our lives to drive to, park, re-park, re-re-park, and get the cameras out for this attraction in Rosarito.

What could possibly follow coastal soft porn? Matt says we've got to see the beach horses next.

"Okay, let's go see the beach horses," we say, grudgingly going along, sad to see the boobies disappearing in the distance.

What would you do if your neighbor's house received this boob job?

I have to admit the horses are wonderful to see, and the overlook where they roam is breathtaking. We stop awhile and enjoy the view.

Suddenly, we are all starving—again. I know why, and I'll say this: when hangover hunger strikes, it is vital to address the malady promptly. If not speedily addressed, hanger will set it. Hanger is a cross between hunger and anger, which, if left untreated, may result in pouting, stomping of feet, insults or hurtful words. We decide raw oysters on the half shell with french fries will be our remedy du jour since we didn't get any yesterday.

Matt guides us to a restaurant on the water in the fisherman's village. Up the stairs and onto a rickety wooden deck we go, sit, and take our medicine. As we watch the waves form, we notice two whales heading north just past the break. It's an amazing sight we appreciate silently. Just kidding.

"I wonder where those two are off to?" I say.

"Happy hour!" someone jokes.

Friends out on the road stopping to see the horses.

We almost choke on oysters as we crack up, picturing the whales bellying up to the bar. "Wait. What if they take up the whole bar? We better get going!"

That's when we remember there is a big beach bar just north of our bungalow. Thank you, Mr. and Mrs. Whale, for reminding us! I know it is probably sacrilege to be thinking of the next bar while something as wonderful as migrating whales are in front of your nose. What are you going to do? It's not like we have a schedule. We are who we are. And, we do think the whales are pretty cool.

Below the restaurant is a beautiful beach and a cove full of fishermen's tents and tables set

The beach at a fisherman's village south of Rosarito, Mexico.

up to sell their catch of the day. There is a man casting his fishing pole from a jetty, and a seal in the water that eats the fish before the fish can take the bait. The seal waits. The man casts. The fish chases the lure. The seal eats. Repeat. We are completely entertained through at least three rounds of this natural theater.

On the way back to the bungalow, Matt pulls off the road a few times to show me some fun surf breaks, but we don't dare attempt to paddle out and surf even though we both have our boards with us. When the heavy rains fall near the coastal areas, the flooding in the streets picks up fecal coliform—poop, to the layperson—and that flows directly into the ocean. When these levels are too high, the beaches are closed to swimming and surfing, and that's what's happened here. So, we watch the waves from our poop-free vantage points and fantasize about taking the lefts or rights (wave directions), then go to our bungalow to drop off the car and walk down the beach to a popular bar called Papas.

We're faced with a major obstacle on our stroll, though. The runoff from the heavy rains has turned into a small river splitting the beach, running between us and our drinks. Our trek seems doomed. How will we cross? We can take off our shoes and socks, roll our pants up, and wade across. After all, it isn't deep. However, it is a river of raw sewage—"Poop River" we dub it. How to cross Poop River?

Aha! There are old planks and big rocks lying around on the beach. Let's build a bridge! We gather our construction materials and begin constructing. As we look over to the mouth of the river, we see several locals wading across barefoot.

"Ewwww!" we say in unison as we watch in horror. Imagine poop squishing through your toes! Gag! "Ewwww!"

Rumor has it that, in retaliation for US plans for a border wall, the Mexican government deliberately opens up the sewage systems to let them flow into the ocean. I guess the plan is for the raw sewage to flow north from the Tijuana area into the San Diego area. That would have been a pretty devious way of protesting the wall—forcing those in Southern California to swim in poop. The problem is the currents flow south during the rainy season; so, even if the plan was real, it would have only succeeded in polluting Mexican beaches part of the year.

In any event, we succeed in crossing Poop River by hopping on the rocks and planks we have so artfully positioned. We are architects! We are proud! We make it in time for "beer-thirty" at Papas!

After Papas, we do a little shopping, and then it's time to prepare for our lobster dinner at Puerto Nuevo, a restaurant famous for its views and large portions. Matt whets our appetites with his descriptions of the homemade jalapeño biscuits and butter served with every entree.

The outside deck sits directly over the breaking waves. We are perched safe and high on the pilings, but the sound is deep and thundering as the waves pound the bulkheads. The dining area is enclosed in plexiglass to limit the evening air's chill.

Drip. Drip. Splash.

Our table is against the window, providing amazing views of the sunset. I keep noticing little white specks appearing on the table. I wipe them away, but they reappear—splash. The spots are wet and speckled with black. I start to think it's pepper from somewhere. Oh well, back to our dinner conversation and surrounding scenery. We watch the birds fly over the breaking waves and catch little fish. Then they return to their nest of shrieking baby birds and feed them.

Drip. Drip. Splash.

More white and black spots are on the table. More shrieking of baby birds. Those birds are loud. They sound close. Where the hell is their nest that they sound so close? Answer. Right above my head, in the rafters holding up the plexiglass! Those little black and white specks dripping and splashing our table are baby bird shit!

"Ewwwww!" we all say in unison.

Splash, and then plop! That shit lands right in my water glass.

In broken Spanish, we explain there is caca coming from the ceiling and landing in my water. I think a few of those splashes bounce off the table and hit me in the teeth while I'm laughing.

"Ewwwww!" Gag.

We move tables.

The lobster dinners arrive and we feast, laugh, drink and eat the jalapeño biscuits to our hearts' content.

No phones or devices are present at this dinner among friends, and no baby birds are harmed during the recording of this story.

We survive the crossing of Poop River in time for happy hour.

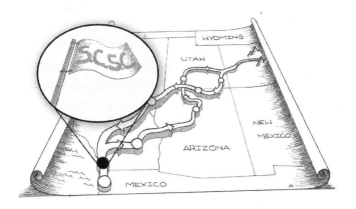

Day Nine
You Shall Not Pass

"Every day is a journey, and the journey itself
is home."

—Matsuo Bashō,
*Narrow Road to the Interior:
And Other Writings*

May 9, 2017
Destination: America

Car packed. Copilot on board. Maps accessible.
Leftover beer and tequila in the trunk.

We begin our drive back to the United States.
The ride is beautiful, enjoyable, and smooth
until the signs leading us to I-5 disappear. We're

pretty sure we've somehow instead gotten ourselves on the road to Tijuana.

Boom! Pothole. Beep beep!

As you may remember, we were strongly advised to stay away from Tijuana with a new car. And, now we are in Tijuana. Oh boy. Let's just say that driving is creative here.

Boom! Pothole. Beep beeeeep!

We make a quick decision. My copilot fires up the rusty browser on her cell phone and lets Google Maps guide us back to the border. It's only the second time we have had to resort to an app, and we decide it is okay for our stats and averages. For everything there is a season, and getting lost on a bumpy road leading who knows where in Mexico qualifies as one of those moments! Turn, turn, turn.

Boom! Beep!

Before too long, we slow down and join the long line of cars waiting to go through customs. While we're stuck in line, dozens of street vendors wind their way through the cars selling everything from giant yard sculptures of turtles to ukuleles. The turtle is tempting, and Kristy decides she needs a ukulele just after the salesman has disappeared into the sea of vendors. I come to my senses and realize a yard turtle the size of a kayak may not be the best idea, given that we can neither fit it in nor on the car. We settle for two Coca-Colas. Our friends have told us it's made using real sugar in Mexico instead of the fake sugar in American

Coke. Old-school. We don't know if it's the power of suggestion or the real thing, but the Coke today sure seems to taste better—more natural.

We hit the front of the line—time for the interrogation. "What was your purpose for visiting Mexico?" "How long did you stay?" "Oh wait, you're from Colorado?"

Oh boy, here we go, I think. Profiled at the border because of my Colorado license plates. I interviewed my brother, Charlie, on license plate profiling for my first book, Weedgalized in Colorado: True Tales from the High Country. It's kind of surreal to realize it is happening to me now.

The border guard mentions something about my license plate and then asks me if I know it is illegal to transport marijuana for any reason, including medical, into the United States. I'm so tempted to say, "Hey detective, think about it. Why would I bring Mexican weed back to Colorado?" Talk about bringing sand to the beach!

Some of the world's best scientists and horticulturalists are in Colorado, growing the finest strains known to (this) man, but I guess Mexican swag weed is still popular after all these years. We loved it growing up. It

Road trip photo worthy signage.

was cheap, and the joints would sometimes pop like popcorn from an undiscovered seed. "Seed weed," we called it.

Pop!

The guards instruct us to pull into the search bay, and we are told to wait for the canine unit. I am fine with that; we had already gotten rid of any pot that may have found its way into our trunk on our travels. Then I begin to think, "What if there were some crumbs of weed under the seats from our legal purchases in Colorado?" Oh well, I guess we'll find out. I'm not very worried.

After a few more questions from some of the higher-ranking guards, they conclude we are not transporting marijuana, even with the big WEEDGALIZED.COM banner sticker across the back windshield. They do a search of the trunk and back seat and don't see any contraband. We must have been under the legal limit for leftover beer and tequila. The dogs are never summoned. They return our passports and wave us on.

On to America

Today is our last day to apply the thirty bucks we paid to drive through Zion National Park to the annual national parks pass, so we're on the hunt for a national park as soon as we cross the border. Time to take out our trusty map.

Recalling our loosely-planned return route devised before leaving Arizona, we locate Cabrillo National Monument on our map. It looks like it's somewhat on our way to our next stop—surfing near San Diego—so we follow the off-highway roads and find our way there.

It's a success! Great views of San Diego from Cabrillo's overlooks. It's hard to explain how exhilarating it is to travel flexibly, altering the course as we go, wandering on our own timeline (unless we're accidentally headed to Tijuana). Everything you see feels like a bonus and blessing in one. There will be more serendipity ahead on this trip.

California coastal view from a Cabrillo Monument viewpoint.

Kristy and Johnny's 5 Fun Facts

1. The site commemorates Juan Rodriguez Cabrillo's 1542-1543 expedition aboard San Salvador into what is now San Diego Bay.
2. It is the first European exploration of the west coast of the United States.
3. In 1913, President Woodrow Wilson creates the Cabrillo National Monument
4. The view of San Diego is said to be the finest harbor view in the United States.

5. It's known as San Diego's Hometown National Park.

Arriving at Cardiff by the Sea aka Cardiff and The SCSC—The Summit County Surf Club

I'm in a surf club in Colorado; there are twelve of us and growing. I know, it sounds odd. It could be considered a support group for wave withdrawal. We're a bunch of old surfers who mostly grew up in a coastal area where surfing was a huge part of our lives. We meet weekly at happy hours, commiserate about our landlocked status, and plan at least one San Diego surfing trip each year. We have a great time.

You guessed it. Kristy and I are now on our way to this year's annual surfing trip, planned since last year as the foundation of our technology detox travel itinerary.

Each trip has its own array of characters. Over the years, Summit County Surf Club members have invited friends and family and friends of friends; so, by now, each roster includes people from all over the country and usually one or two people I've never met. The dynamic is always different, so each year is a new adventure.

Here's this year's cast:

Neal is from New Jersey, lives in Colorado, and is a short-haired version of Jeff Spicoli from Fast Times at Ridgemont High. He brings an official clipboard, sanctioned at a prior vote, to record SCSC meeting minutes and plans.

Mark is Neal's older brother and also lives in Colorado. He's responsible for Neal learning to swim at a young age. Mark introduced him to the pool when he wasn't looking.

Gunner—Gunnah to New Englanders—is new to surfing. Gunner has a cackle laugh and Heat Miser haircut.

Max is a well-traveled outdoor enthusiast from Breckenridge, Colorado. He manages a restaurant called Ember.

CJ is from San Clemente, California, and now lives in Colorado. He is a top contender in our annual beach bocce tournament. Picture a tall Malibu Ken doll with long hair.

Horse is a US Marine, living and working near San Diego. He is CJ's cousin-in-law. I say US Marine even though he is retired. Try telling a marine he's retired! Horse has been kind enough to lend us many surfboards over the years. He usually shows up at our campsite with several gallons of hot brewed coffee at 5:00 a.m.

Johnny Day is Gunner's brother who lives in Santa Barbara, California. He attends annually and is the reigning beach bocce champion and keeper (for now) of the prestigious trophy.

Kristy Marie Smith is from Arkansas, and lives in Colorado. This trip will be her first attempt at surfing.

There are nine of us, counting me. As you already know, I am from New Jersey—South Jersey to be specific, not shoobie-ville like Neal and Mark—and now reside in Colorado.

A two-hour drive from Cabrillo and we're there: the gorgeous beachside surfing campground in San Elijo State Park! We're the last to arrive, and it immediately feels like we're kids at summer camp again, with so many adventures and possibilities ahead of us. We're all excited, happy to be off work and away from home with nothing but our tents.

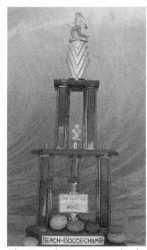

The Beach Bocce trophy in all its glory.

Smartphones are nowhere to be found. We disconnect from the world and reconnect with each other, just us and the surf. A sacred bond is usually formed during these trips, leaving us forever changed—like in *Stand by Me* or *The Goonies*.

People are unpacking, icing down coolers of beer, and setting up tents. Neal has his trusty clipboard, paper, and pen and accompanies me to discuss parking passes with the park ranger; we have too many vehicles. The first one is included and the second must pay. The limit is two vehicles. Any extras must park outside the campground. It's a good thing Neal has his clipboard. He is so official and is my parking hero. People treat you differently when you have one under your arm. Try it and see.

Back at camp, settled in, we all introduce ourselves since there's always a new guy or gal. New gear is brought out for an evening of show and tell and, sometimes, applause. Who has a new wetsuit, leash, surfboard, or board bag? We are an appreciative audience. We get comfortable in our regulation beach chairs, complete with requisite beer holders in the armrests, and we relax by the fire.

The first night tends to be mellow as we anticipate the morning surf session—the reason we are all here. Surrounding a campfire, we enjoy turkey sandwiches, whiskey, tequila, and beer; then down to beach to listen to the waves we go. Finally, one by one, the fellowship of the Summit County Surf Club retires to tents to sleep.

Kristy is the last one up, and Neal makes official note of it on the clipboard.

Johnny's Surf Terminology

Get ready! In the next few chapters we're surfing and using surfer lingo. Here's the essential terminology, as I define it, for your surfer 101 cheat sheet:

point break
a place in the ocean where a wave hits the bottom, then breaks in each direction

party wave
two or more surfers, usually friends, riding the same wave close together

position
the surfer closest to the wave's peak has right
of way

shred or shred it up
a surfer's ability to turn the board in all directions
on a wave and stay on for a long ride

chest-high waves
waves as high as an average man's chest when
one is up and riding on them, measured from the
bottom of the wave

head-high waves
waves as high as an average man's head,
measured from the bottom of the wave (There can
also be knee-high, waist-high, overhead, double-
overhead, etc.)

chest- to head-high waves
the temptation to make chest-high waves bigger
when you're telling your surfing story, like the fish
that got away and the one you caught that was,
"This Big!"

shore break
waves that break where the water meets the sand
and can't be ridden with a surfboard

shoobie
a term used in New Jersey to describe someone
who lives more than a thirty-minute drive from the
beach, synonymous with tourist

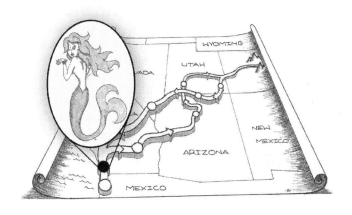

Day Ten
Not Only That...

"No, the thing is, we all love storytelling, and as a
writer you get to tell stories all the time."
—Joyce Carol Oates

May 10, 2017
Destination: Cardiff by the Sea

The best part about these trips is there is never
an agenda. We surf, sit on the beach and watch
our buddies surf, hang out at camp, or go across
the tracks to eat, stroll, or shop. Those are the
only options, and we don't need anything else.

Today, Neal plans a long walk with Kristy
and me along the beach to the next town over,
Encinitas. The tide low, it is perfect for a beach

hike. We stroll along, the sun above us and the breeze straight off the ocean, collecting cool shells and stones along the way. Time passes as slowly as we stroll. Some of the deepest conversations about life can be had during these moments—gems of time.

Rules and Rituals

Cool beach walks. Cold beer. Great food. Old and new friends. Over the years, our surf club has boiled life down to its simple pleasures. While we're relaxing together on this second day of our trip, let me tell you more about our discoveries and traditions we've developed along the way.

The Train Track Rule

All participants in our surf trips must agree to follow one golden rule—pretty much our only regulation—the Train Track Rule. Group members who leave the campground and cross the nearby railroad tracks are advised not to return empty-handed. Making it across the tracks means you have reached the little town across the highway where supplies are plentiful and cheap; and you are, therefore, required to bring back at least one of these top three items on the surfer survival list:

- Firewood
- Ice
- Beer

Paper Maps, No Apps

TIP / Before leaving the campground, take a quick inventory on what supplies are low. If you are price savvy, you are free to purchase the least expensive commodity to satisfy the "Train Track Rule".

Fail to bring back at least one of these vital items and face the consequences; you must purchase one at a premium price at the campground store, and you may even be ridiculed and teased at the next sanctioned surf meeting. Neal has been known to give out demerits during story time around the campfire, too.

I have taken drastic measures to avoid that humiliation, not always with the best results. A couple of years ago, abiding by the Train Track Rule, I purchased a thirty-pack of beer. After exiting the store, I hoisted the case onto my shoulder; it broke apart, and beer cans flew in every direction. If that wasn't embarrassing enough, some of the flying cans landed on the cop car parked in front of the store. Everyone nearby rushed to my aid and scrambled to collect the rolling cans of Pabst Blue Ribbon. I couldn't stop laughing as I chased the two cans that made it under the cop car. The officer was not present, so we got away with this inadvertent vandalism, but I'd still take a fine over a Neal campfire humiliation any day of the week.

Bad Juju

Saying the s-word is bad juju for surfers. It can jolt us out of the best of moods—temporarily, anyway. Here's what that looks like.

Today, we work up quite an appetite on our beach stroll to Encinitas, so we make our way to the Ale House (imagine that) where we can satisfy our hunger and thirst for cold local brew. As usual, we strike up a conversation with the bartender, who is also a surfer. Neal loves to get to know the locals and tell them about our dynamic group and our landlocked Colorado surf club.

I don't know how the conversation shifts from snowboarding the Rockies to great white shark sightings, but it does. The week prior, a girl was bitten in the thigh at a nearby surf break. The bartender tells us a dead whale washed up a few weeks ago. Instead of hauling the carcass twenty miles out to sea, the coast guard only towed it two miles. The locals believe that's why so many sightings have been reported.

We all stare at different focal points for a moment and then simultaneously sip our beers. Awkward silence. Fear. Pause. More sips. "How about that game last week?" seems like the next logical topic.

The bartender meanders away, and Kristy, Neal and I chuckle at what just happened. Neal suspects this local is just trying to scare some tourists from paddling out. Shoobies are used to that. It doesn't matter to me, but I prefer not to hear these stories. Surfers do not like the s-word.

We learned after our trip there were fifteen documented shark sightings nearby the week we all surfed.

The Mommy Parade

Every morning, at approximately the same time, there is a group of twelve to fifteen young moms who work out, pushing their newborns in strollers. Dressed in their fancy workout clothes, complete with headbands, they speed walk or jog to each of the dozen or so staircases spread along the coastal town. There is an entrance to the beach every few blocks or so. The campground is on the same level as the highway and sits atop the bluffs. Each staircase goes down to the beach. From the bluff one can see the coast line in each direction. We watch as they park all the strollers at the top of the stairs. One of the moms stays to watch all the babies while the rest run down the stairs (approximately 160 steps), touch the beach sand, and run back up the stairs. We guess they take turns watching the babies, so they all get an equal workout. Yes, we enjoy watching the mommy parade. You know what they say about California girls.

Food and Drink

Part of being on vacation is researching and discovering fun places to eat and drink. Coming back to the campground with a new restaurant discovery elevates one's social status in the surf club.

Pipes Cafe

Members of the Summit County Surf Club are creatures of habit, and that is a good thing when it comes to breakfast. Pipes is a little breakfast place that serves up the best surfing fuel one can buy, and it's always packed. The walls are covered, floor to ceiling, with surf photos, autographed pictures, surfboards, and a painted map of the beaches with the names of the breaks. Pipes' staff remembers us every year as "the Colorado crew." Dana, a manager we met many years ago, is still there and wears the biggest smile when she sees us. We eat almost every breakfast at Pipes during our trips here and sometimes go back for more after an early morning surf session. Their egg sandwich is our favorite.

VG Donut & Bakery and the Rare and Elusive Buttercream-filled Donut

The most amazing donut ever created can be found at VG Donut & Bakery in Cardiff, California, if you're very, very lucky. This donut is rarely available and possibly magic. It is chocolate-iced and resembles a Boston cream-filled donut; but, instead of the yellow custard, it's filled with white buttercream to the point that it almost takes the shape of an overinflated football. Should I make the joke about Boston and football inflation issues? "If Tom Brady's football wasn't this full, he never would have gotten in trouble!" Maybe not, someone in New England might be reading.

We discovered this elusive treat accidentally when fortune smiled upon us two years ago and we picked up a dozen donuts to bring back to camp. I did not see the donut in the store—I swear, none of us did—yet back at camp, I reached into the bag and pulled it out. Everyone stopped and stared. What was this alien treat? Where did it come from? Had I won Willy Wonka's golden ticket?

Things were a bit foggy that night; I can't imagine why. I may or may not have held the donut above the fire while everyone watched in awe, mouths open and drooling. We agreed that whatever this thing was, it was as rare and exciting as a Bigfoot sighting.

Silence. I ate the donut. Yes, it was as heavenly as we had all anticipated. I did not share. Would you? We all soon fell into a deep slumber—possibly under the spell of the donut—like hobbits by the fire. The next morning we awoke by the firepit and felt we had dreamt the event. Nobody spoke of this magic for quite some time.

The Cardiff Office

There are not many bars near the campground, but one we frequent is the Office. Every year we joke about having to go to the office to do paperwork, our code for going to have a couple of beers on tap. I wonder how many surfers in surrounding campsites over the many years have made that same joke.

Johnny Welsh

The bartender, Mike—originally from Boston—remembers us each year. This year we meet Heidie, another bartender. Tonight, Kristy and I arrive early evening, missing the first of the big surfing collisions during the evening session. While Kristy and I are making our way through office paperwork, Johnny Day and Neal crash mid-wave, causing a game-ending injury to the longboard we call the Green Machine. Johnny Day and Neal are uninjured but unhappy. They join us at the Office; and together, we drink to the recuperation of the Green Machine, now awaiting surgery at the surf repair shop. To have a surfboard out of commission during a trip brings tears to our eyes.

We've spent many an evening at the Office, oftentimes staying late enough to make the next morning's surf session sting. Ocean water is the closest thing to a cure for a hangover I know of, but sometimes the Office gets best of me.

Story Time

The campfire is the pulpit where the stuff of legends are told—surf stories of years past, like epic waves and surf sessions. The day at Cottons is one of our favorites.

Cottons

It was a bright and early morning session after Halloween night. We hiked about a half hour down the beach to paddle out to the surf break called Cottons, south of San Clemente. The shore break was monstrous, crashing on the beach like thunder and shaking the ground.

I kept smelling beer and whiskey as I paddled out, and was confused. Was it my own breath, or was the smell coming from CJ, twenty yards ahead? Sometimes the late night campfire antics are still in our systems early mornings, i.e. booze. As we paddled out, we could see dolphins swimming through the chest- to head-high waves before they broke.

Neal's permanent expression of stoke.

Neal says the best wave he ever saw me on was that day at Cottons. He was paddling back out and I caught a decent-sized wave and turned left. He said my eyes were as big as Frisbees as I dragged my back hand on the wave and let out a little high pitched, "Yeww!"

I think his eyes may have bigger than mine. When it comes to Neal and surfing, camping, drinking, or just about anything, he is always running on pure stoke. For all of us, though, it's almost as much fun watching our buddies catch good waves as catching them ourselves.

That same day, Gunner caught his first waves ever. CJ and I were on a party wave, Johnny Day shredded it up, and Gunner and I saw a sea turtle pop his head up in front of us!

We still don't know if the mermaid was real.

The Mermaid

Alana Blanchard once said, "Surfer girls rip and they are hot." One mid-morning session—when Neal and I went alone—would forever be etched in our minds as the mermaid sighting. The waves were small, fun, clean, and about knee- to waist-high. There were very few surfers out, and Neal and I were enjoying the little waves and usual conversation in the lineup. Then, out of nowhere, a girl paddled out. I swear we thought she was a mermaid! She was beautiful and confident and refreshing to see on Old Man's Break. She dunked her long golden hair into the ocean and shook it out from side to side. Was she real?

Neal, being the smooth cat he is, noticed she was wearing a watch. "Hey Johnny, do you happen to know what time it is?" he asked me, knowing full well I don't wear a watch.

"Nah, probably getting close to 11:00 a.m."

"Oh, hi guys, I have the time," said a mystical voice from the deep.

It was her: the mermaid. She spoke to us!

We said hello and Neal gave her the lowdown of our surf club in Colorado. She smiled, we all surfed, and then she disappeared. We turned to look and did not see her behind us or walking out of the water. We looked again and she wasn't on the beach or the stairs going up. I'm still not convinced this event happened or she was human.

Games and Inventions

I find it rather amusing what the mind will do when free of distractions. Our idle minds like to create silly games and nonsensical ideas around the campfire.

Synonymous

There's a vocabulary game we play anytime we get together. Whenever a big word pops up in one of our many conversations, someone else must immediately say, "Not only that, but it's_____," filling in the blank with a synonym, as if they don't know what the original word means. Trust me, it's funnier than you think.

It all started when I was bartending in Destin, Florida, many years back. One night, after getting our asses kicked by the dinner rush, I was in the mood to make strong drinks. The sous-chef, Scott O'Daniel, came up to the bar and ordered a Captain and coke. I make a strong one.

Later that evening, when the chef was feeling good, he said, "Damn, you should have seen the first drink Johnny Welsh made me. There was so much rum it was translucent!"

I immediately responded, "Not only that...you could see through it!"

O'Daniel spit up half his drink, laughing so hard the booze shot out of his nose. So now, whenever a big word is thrown out, we all try to top each other by being the first to say, "Not only that..." The more complex the word and the quicker the rebuttal, the funnier.

 The trick is not to overplay it or try to define a common word. Wait for the right moment, when nobody is expecting it, and unleash the sarcasm. Ah, to be puerile forever. Not only that, it's nice to act immature!

The Squirrel Launcher

On my first surf trip seven years ago, we had a problem with ground squirrels at the campsite. There were so many, and they loved to steal our snacks. Even in the daytime, they were not shy about invading our picnic table.

I proposed the invention of the squirrel launcher: a catapult with a small net and bait inside. The net would be attached to large rubber bands like a water balloon launcher. The squirrel taking the bait would trigger the release and bam! The squirrel would go flying out of the campsite, over the fence, past the

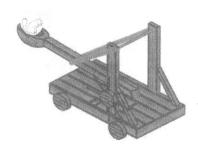

Early prototype of squirrel launcher.

bluffs, and into the ocean. I figured the water would be a soft enough landing it wouldn't kill the squirrel if it knew how to swim. Of course, then we began to imagine ourselves out surfing in the lineup, suddenly seeing a big splash.

"What was that?" one of us would say.

Another would respond, "We got one! We got a squirrel!"

We never had time to build the contraption, which was a good thing since it might have put us all in jail for violating animal rights. But, you have to admit, it's a hilarious image. No squirrels were harmed during this brainstorming session.

Neal's Surfboard Rack

Neal designed and built a rack that holds surfboards a few inches above the sand to keep the boards' wax grit-free. He used PVC piping he painted blue and made two separate racks, one for the nose and one for the tail. The racks were made to store several boards, and I keep telling him he's got to patent that thing!

One half of Neal's surfboard rack.

Neal's Bocksch Board

I imagine another of Neal's inventions as an As Seen on TV product.

"Ever get too close to the campfire and have no place to put your feet? Tired of hot sneaker syndrome around a metal fire pit? Well, do we have the product for you! Allow us to introduce the Bocksch Board, a fireproof footrest to place anywhere between you and the fire. It even

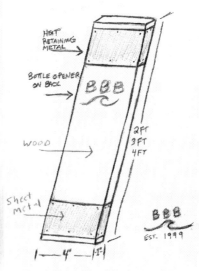

Early sketch of Neal's Bocksch Board (patent pending).

has straps for your feet (and, on one model, a built-in bottle-opener, too). It's so compact it can fit under your car seat; and, if you act now, we'll throw in an extra set of neon foot straps. Wait! There's more! Act in the next half hour and you can score two Bocksch Boards for the price of one! That's right, for one low payment of $49.95, you get two Bocksch Boards and an extra set of neon straps!"

PS Bocksch is Neal's last name, pronounced "Bosh."

Moth in the Ear, Mouse in the Shoe

The ideas I come up with at the campfire always involve pranks I'd like to play; that's who I am. I tell my fellow surfers—maybe even every year—I want to invent a gadget that sounds like a bumble bee or a moth to flutter near a friend's ear, making them flinch, duck, scream, or run. Funny, right? Yeah, the Colorado surfers didn't think so either.

How about this: a fake mouse you can make wiggle through a remote control, perfectly sized to fit in your pal's shoe? No?

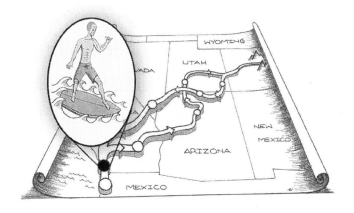

Day Eleven
Stewart Goes to the Hospital

"I do write a lot from personal experience, but I also embellish a bit."

—Miranda Lambert

May 11, 2017
Location: Still Cardiff

The Stewart is a surfboard, a longboard to be exact: nine feet of precision in the ocean and a wave-catching machine in the lineup. We all want to be the surfer on the Stewart, but the boards are first come, first serve at the campsite. Those who wake up earliest get first pick from the quiver. CJ, an early riser and a tall drink of water, likes a longer board. He is particularly partial to the Stewart.

Today, part of the team plans to surf Swami's, a classic point break. It may even be one of the top ten in Southern California. Johnny Day, Gunner, and, of course, CJ rise early and decide to surf this break nearby while the rest of us take our time getting moving. Not long after the late risers have all rolled out of their tents, we see the early birds trudging back to camp looking crestfallen, especially poor CJ.

His voice trembles as he recounts the story of the wounding of the Stewart. CJ and the Stewart were run over by a grumpy older surfer—an unprovoked attack that left CJ with a cut on his ankle and put a big gash in the Stewart, rendering it out of commission for the rest of the trip.

Forget the bloody surfer, is the board gonna make it?

This is a tragedy! As CJ describes the event, I imagine the scene. I see medics carrying away the Stewart on a stretcher, leaving CJ bleeding in ankle deep water. I picture the waves hitting his body and rinsing blood back into the ocean like a scene from Jaws. Anyway, I snap out of it and offer my deepest sympathy for the Stewart's—I mean—CJ's tragedy.

That sad tale makes us hungry. The wind has come up and the waves are blown out. It's too windy for surfing, so an afternoon session isn't going to happen. Eating is always a great Plan B for this group.

Bull Taco is the campground's food emporium, and that's where we happily go. When Kristy and I arrive, we're surprised to see a crew from the Travel Channel filming a segment on how delicious these tacos are and how spectacular the ocean view is from the outside tables. Or, maybe we're not so surprised: Bull Taco tacos are amazing.

Before we can even sit down, a Travel Channel crew member asks us to sign waivers, allowing them to film us while we eat. Yes! Of course! (As you have probably figured out by now, we are not shy. Still, it's hard to eat without laughing with a giant camera zoomed in on your face.) We do our best to act casual and chew normally. I think I may be snotting myself on camera trying not to laugh. I can hear the talent scouts and casting directors calling me now, "Let's get that snot guy for our next movie!"

We usually surf in the evening, but today it's still too windy, so we stay on the beach for happy hour and sunset watching. Kristy suggests we shoot jump photos, and we're all up for it. We take great individual pictures and a keepsake group photo, not a smartphone in sight.

CJ claims to have
the most air in these
jump photos

Mad Max with a
smile ear to ear

Johnny Day as da
Vinci's Vitruvian Man

Me way up there. I think I'm a half inch higher than CJ.

The Bocksch brothers in unison

Kristy, the one who led the charge for the jump photos

Gunner, free as a bird!

After our photo shoot, I decide it's time to share my big surprise. I deftly shift the conversation to Tastykake Butterscotch Krimpets.

"Hey, have you guys ever had a Tastykake?" I ask. Tastykake Butterscotch Krimpets are only made and sold on the East Coast; you can find them in Philly, New York, Delaware and New Jersey. These sweets taste kind of like Hostess Twinkies but with butterscotch icing on top and no filling.

Neal and I explain just how prized Tastykakes are on the East Coast. We share stories of hoarding the treats to trade during lunch at elementary school. You do not want to be the kid with nothing in your brown bag lunch to trade. Apples aren't going to cut it, nor will Chips Ahoy cookies (although one kid tried to trade his apple every single lunch). Tastykakes hold all the value.

Jersey kids know the right way to eat a Tastykake. You can't just open it and eat it. You have to rub the plastic wrapper back and forth, facedown, on the lunch table. This allows for a release of the sticky sugar icing from the wrapper. Holding up a clean wrapper for approval after the Tastykake has been extracted gets rewarded with smiles and pats on the back.

Just when our audience believes we have exhausted our Tastykake tribute (or maybe is exhausted by our Tastykake tribute), I present my surprise with a big flourish: my own brown bag full of Tastykake Butterscotch Krimpets for the whole surf crew.

Do you know how hard it is to transport delights on a road trip with a person who gets hungry every twenty miles (meaning me)? My willpower even astounds me, but it was bolstered by the anticipation of this very moment. Those Tastykakes traveled to Vegas, to Mexico, and back with us, unbitten. (No worries about spoilage: Tastykakes have a shelf life, similar to Twinkies, of a few hundred years or so.)

That night, Kristy and I go back to the Office, and yes, I am still hungry for sweets, so we stop by VG Donut & Bakery. Lightning strikes twice! First Tastykakes and now the elusive white buttercream-filled donut is in the store, begging for my consumption! I cannot say no. I buy it, take it back to the Office, and eat it at the bar with my eyes closed.

The rest of our crew shows up after dinner, exhausted. They go back early to the campsite and light a fire but then decide to douse it and go to sleep. Kristy and I return a few hours later, relight the fire and burn the rest of the wood.

The next morning, they couldn't figure out how all the wood had been burned. We awake to them blaming each other, and we can't stop laughing.

Summit County Surf Club group photo 2017, Cardiff by the Sea

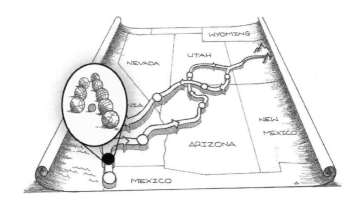

Day Twelve
Veni, Vidi, Vici

"Our battered suitcases were piled on the sidewalk again; we had longer ways to go. But no matter, the road is life."

—Jack Kerouac, *On the Road*

May 12, 2017
Destination: South Campsite

Today we must change campsites. Our current site isn't available tonight, so we have to break camp, check out by 11:00 a.m., and then wait until 3:00 p.m. before checking in at our next site since it needs to be cleaned.

Today is Kristy's day, a day I know she'll always remember: she will attempt to surf for the first time.

Johnny Welsh

We, as experienced surfers, get a special feeling in our hearts when we see someone paddling out for the first time; it reminds us of our first try. We're moved even more when we see someone stand up and ride their first wave.

Today turns out to be doubly special for Kristy and those of us watching her because she tries, and she succeeds—mostly. She stands up and rides six waves all the way in! Well, she doesn't actually ride the face of the wave—she rides the white water—but this is still a great accomplishment.

I help her by standing in chest-deep water, selecting waves and pushing her board. Wave number one: nose dive. Wave number two: she stands up and rides the white water a good distance!

What makes her first wave sweeter is the audience. Our beach chairs are set up in our usual configuration for happy hour, and most of the guys are watching and cheering. Kristy is on cloud nine and hooked on the sport. She beams ear to ear.

Later, we sit, enjoy some cold beers, and have deep conversations: philosophy o'clock. The topic du jour is naming the various ways we end our rides on the waves. I know, I know: it's so profound. Every ride must come to an end, and endings are not exactly elegant, no matter how beautiful or long the ride. You know how gymnasts dismount after a routine: arms raised, chest out, ready for applause? Surfers' dismounts are...different. Each is unique; each deserves a name. Tonight, we come up with the following labels:

Mark performing the always bold, "Hit the deck" dismount.

Gunner performing the death-defying starfish dismount.

Mark on a front-side old school belly flop maneuver.

Gunner, in an effort to out perform The Starfish, pulls off the Ghost-Rider.

Neal with his classic dismount that started classification process, "The Neal Dismount"

Johnny performing the rare and accidental, "The Sinker" A.K.A. "Where's My Wave?"

Paper Maps, No Apps

It's our last full day at the beach—but never fear—our crew has perfected the art of the vacation finale. We know how to end a fantastic trip with a memorable bang, full of ritual and ridiculousness. The first event of the final day: the bocce tournament.

We don't take this sport lightly. Our tournament has multiple heats, elaborate double elimination rules, and even a loser bracket. We have arrived at the semifinals. It's Neal against Gunner.

Neal is on his last throw. This ball has to land closest to the white target ball if he is to make the finals. He pauses. He concentrates. He throws. The ball arcs high in the air, looking like it's in slow motion, and then thud! It lands next to the target.

Neal begins his celebration. Picture those wide circling arcs soccer players run on the field after scoring a goal. This is Neal, running far and wide, his hands in the victory pose. We aren't sure, but we all think we hear him yelling in Latin, "Veni, vidi, vici!"

Neal doesn't realize that he has not yet won. Gunner still has a turn, and he's standing there— one ball in his left hand—patiently waiting for Neal to stop the shenanigans and get out of the way. Neal stops, flabbergasted that the game is not over. He does not see the last ball in Gunner's hand.

Gunner throws. The ball hangs in the air in the highest arc we have ever seen. It lands closer to the target than Neal's. Neal has not made the finals and falls to his knees in agony. He sits in the sand for a while, arms outstretched and facing the heavens. He yells, "Whyyyyyy?"

CJ eventually wins the coveted trophy in the final match against Gunner, but the trophy has to stay in California. Sanctioned games for the trophy transfer happen only at the fall tournament. It is written on the clip board.

The joke of the day quickly becomes the theme jingle for ESPN. "And in today's sports news, Neal Bocksch runs amok in a premature celebration that ends in agony for him as he is knocked out of the semifinals!" followed by "Dah Dah Dah, Dah Dah Dah."

 TIP Make sure you are paying close attention to a Beach Bocce Ball tournament. (Especially if you are one of the players competing.) Ah-hem, Neal!.

After bocce, we head to the beach for mini-surf sessions, which go great until we are interrupted by a brat pack, screaming and yelling and dropping in on each other and just being disrespectful to the surf gods.

Neal is run out of the water by this gang. CJ isn't impressed with them either and paddles to shore. Johnny Day decides to teach the kids a lesson. He spies one of their leashless boards floating loose and rescues it. Then he runs with it past the lifeguard stand a few hundred yards away and leaves it. A surfboard without a leash can be dangerous to other surfers on a crowded surf break.

Our growing irritation is good sign it's time to

head back and out to our annual last supper at Best Pizza and Brew. We share the best stories of our time together here. Neal recognizes our waitress, Kealey; she photobombed one of our shots a few years ago. We take more photos with Kealey.

Dinner runs late, and we're locked out of our new campsite, blocked by a ten foot high chain-link fence that was closed at 7:00 p.m. We have no choice but to climb the fence and jump over. Each of us has his own distinct style worthy of its own good-natured ribbing from the audience.

Gunner wins again. He is stuck on top of the fence, and we're all laughing too hard to help him. For a good five minutes, Gunner is also laughing too hard to save himself, but he finally extricates himself and jumps down. Our final night's escapades still aren't over, though.

You might think our climbing misadventure would have soured us on the idea of more climbing, but the steep bluff behind the lifeguard shack is just too tempting. We spill up the hill like some sort of giant surfer amoeba, yelling into the wind and laughing for no reason, and I suspect there was also some dancing.

When we get back to the campsite, we play a few final games:

- campfire log balancing
- Hula-Hoop contest with Kristy's rainbow LED Hula-Hoop
- paper airplane flying distance competition

Johnny Welsh

We are all glad to see the next morning that we have photographic evidence of our climb and the campsite games, as none of us remember much of the night.

The beauty of this crew is eagerness to jump in wholeheartedly to the silliest competitions. We all know without saying that day-to-day life is full of serious obligations and concerns, yet we understand the value of letting go and having fun. We dive into each ridiculous project as if it's exactly what we had been waiting to do. Disconnected from apps, we connect with each other in each moment.

An epic ending.

Chris Johnson, Johnny Welsh, and Kristy Smith recapping the trip after midnight.

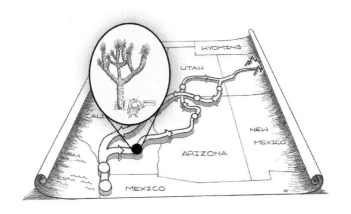

Day Thirteen
That's My Beer

"When I get home I shall write a book about this
place... If I ever do get home."

—Alice,
Alice in Wonderland, 1951

May 13, 2017
Destination: Joshua Tree National Park

One by one, tents are folded up, gear is stowed,
and backpacks are packed. With coffees in hand,
we glance around in silence, looking for forgotten
items, thinking and feeling. The last mornings of
our surf trips are always solemn. Rumor has it
that some of us have even been known to shed a
tear or two.

Surfing commencement: end of a session; beginning of a journey.

On this day, Gunner and CJ hold strong until they see Mark's eyes glistening, and that's it for them. But although we're sad, we all share a secret smile built of a shared journey, a smile full of stories to tell around the next campfire. It's a notch in the belt and another colorful puzzle piece in each of our lives.

I decide to leave my surfboard, the Roland, with Horse. He lives nearby and can store it in his garage, along with his quiver, until the next trip. It goes without saying that if I am unable to attend, the board is there for all to enjoy. This is the highest form of surfer karma.

Since we're driving and the rest of the crew's transportation is scheduled for later that day, Kristy and I are the first to leave. We say our goodbyes and with a blue water ice in hand, we set out to enjoy the gorgeous Pacific Coast

Highway up the coast for a little while. We will drive through five or six coastal towns then turn off and head north on the Five.

Influencing our decision to leave early is the fact that the Stewart Surfboard shop and Pedro's Tacos are just an hour or so up US 101 in San Clemente. Last year, I found the most comfortable pair of Stewart sweat pants at the shop, and I need another pair. Surfer sweatpants are soft and oversized for easy wear after a session.

Oh no! They tell me at the store the company has discontinued the sweats and I'm out of luck. We're on our way out when I get an idea—I need to look through the clearance rack in the back room. Success! Amazing! There is one pair of these pants in the store. They are my size—and half price!

After this arduous shopping excursion, we're craving Pedro's Tacos. CJ introduced us to this famous taco restaurant last year. The classic fish tacos are second to none and we eat them outside on a shiny silver table. Life doesn't get any better.

Back in Colorado, I learn that Neal and Mark had tried to keep the surfing vacation spirit alive all the way home, bringing their leftover beer with them on the train instead of heading to the club car for overpriced brew.

"What's that in your hand sir?"

Neal looks to the left and then to the right as if the conductor simply must be talking to someone else. Then he looks at his hand like he forgot it was attached to his arm.

"That's my beer!" he proudly announces, his head slightly cocked, like a puppy. As if the conductor had gone mad. How dare he? The nerve!

TIP / Try not to bring a beer that is too full on the train. That way you won't lose too much of your investment.

Beer goes away. The ruse doesn't come close to working.

Mark's too honest to try to con the conductor. When he's approached, he lowers his shoulders and says as he surrenders, "Yeah, I guess I have one, too."

Gone. Can't do that. Open containers not allowed.

Another story for next trip's campfire.

US 74 to Lake Elsinore City

Back on the road, we spy a gas station that is absolutely packed with waiting cars. I do a quick calculation. We have a quarter of a tank; we average 40 miles per gallon; and the next gas station must be about thirty miles away, on the other side of the mountain pass. No problem!

Problem. Forty-five minutes of driving uphill on this winding road empties my tank. Oh hell no! We are on a winding mountain road, and the fuel gauge is creeping toward E. I look for any safe place to pull over, but there's nothing but road, mountain, and drop-offs. I now understand why there was such a long line at the gas station prior to the road over the pass.

As the needle drops close and closer to empty, there are still no shoulders to pull over on and no gas stations yet in sight. It will be dangerous as hell to run out of gas on a road like this. The car's running on fumes, and we do not want to be stuck in the middle of this highway! I'm trying to conceive a plan, but my brain is as empty as the tank.

Wait...can it be? Ahead I see a large pull off in the distance, at the top of the pass. I hope we can at least make it there. The gauge is now beyond E, heading toward the steering column.

We make it to the pull off! As we coast in, we see a tow truck loading a corvette at the far end. It looks like

A tow truck with extra gas appears out of thin air.

that driver ran out of gas as well.

I cannot believe this good luck! Something in the universe is looking out for us. I wonder if it's because we forewent the apps for maps!

"How far away is the nearest gas station? My car is out of gas. If it is all downhill from here, maybe we can coast to it?"

"Let me finish loading up this corvette and I will check my tow truck for a spare container of gas."

A few minutes later, the Corvette is secured.

"You're in luck. I have two gallons in the red gas can."

Our situation is now beyond lucky: it's miraculous. The paper map gods are smiling down on us.

Two gallons of gas in the car, and we are back on our road trip with only a fifteen-minute hiccup. How on earth does something like this happen?

The views going down the pass are priceless. Kristy snaps many photos of beautiful Lake Elsinore.

Views of beautiful Lake Elsinore.

We find and turn onto I-15 and locate a gas station before the two gallons run out. We feel very relieved. It's time to figure out where we're going to sleep tonight since the Joshua Tree campground and other campgrounds nearby were already full when we called before our trip.

We decide it might be a good idea to hunt for a campground an hour or so away from Joshua Tree, so we exit at a small town called Indio based on the little tent icon we see by the town on our paper map.

Finding these supposed campgrounds may be another series of adventures! There is nothing on this exit besides a golf course. We stop at the clubhouse which also houses a post office. I don't see how the two correlate.

The guy behind the counter looks at me like I have three heads when I ask if there are any campgrounds in the town.

"Camping? The nerve! Surely they could at least hit a bucket of balls," I imagined the guy thinking.

Joshua Tree National Park

With the search not going well, we decide to forget it for a while and just enjoy Joshua Tree. Maybe we'll find an empty campsite there; you never know. If not, we'll try Twentynine Palms, another city with a little tent icon on our map.

Joshua Tree is national park number three of our bonus trip with the annual pass.

Kristy and Johnny's 5 Fun Facts

1. Joshua Tree boasts a 792,750-acre forest of palm trees, other unusual trees and geological oddities.
2. It was designated a national monument in 1936 and redesignated a national park in 1994.
3. In 1984, it was designated as a Biosphere Reserve.

4. The Mojave Desert and Colorado Desert meet in Joshua Tree National Park.

5. The Joshua tree is a member of the agave family, Yucca brevifolia, not a tree or a cactus.

Don't approach these prickly Cholla cactuses.

Upon arrival, the sign is plain as day at the visitor center: the campgrounds are all full in Joshua Tree. We decide to stick to our plan, though: see the park and deal with lodging later. Unfortunately, this strategy has a low success rate based on past experience, but we are in go mode and we press on to see the landscape.

- Cholla cactus gardens
- Dr Seuss-like trees
- Giant bees
- Cool landscapes
- Martian landscapes and geology
- Joshua Trees

Though we've probably used our paper maps quota of good luck for the day, we decide to check out the campgrounds, hoping someone didn't make it to their campsite and there is one lonely spot for us. Nope.

Scenes like these remind me of a Dr. Seuss book.

At one of the campgrounds, people are filming a music video—or at least that's what it looks like—with sequin jackets, wedding cake, drag makeup, crazy hairdos, and crowns. Did we mistakenly eat a magic cactus? It seems so out of place, like a mirage. Maybe this is how they celebrate having a campsite since it seems like such a hot commodity.

The sun is still up, and we feel a final burst of energy to travel as many miles as the daylight will allow. Onward we go to Twentynine Palms.

Our attempts to explore this town are not fruitful. All the signs are in the wrong places, sending us on a wild goose chase; and, when we stop for directions, the person we ask sends us to a military base. As we pull up, there is a huge security gate allowing access onto the base, but I am not in the mood to have the car searched for clearance. That's not going to happen.

Now, our attempt to leave Twentynine Palms and head for Amboy has failed. I am reminded of Gatlin, a town with no way out, in the movie *Children of the Corn*.

We have trouble fighting the urge to look online for a campground or, worst case, get some hotel prices. We resist and use the old-fashioned drive up and ask system and find a little place with one room left. This must be our stop, so we give up on Amboy for the time being.

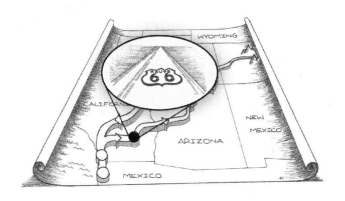

Day Fourteen
Kicks on Route 66

"People don't take trips—trips take people"
—John Steinbeck,
Travels with Charley: In Search of America

May 14, 2017
Destination: Arizona

Our car is parked in a covered carport and I fully appreciate this fact when we see how the morning sun bakes the landscape. Twentynine Palms' climate is considered desert; the nights are cool and the days are hot—oven hot, with dry heat and dust.

I spend the morning cleaning, organizing, and repacking the car to leave the vitals for today's drive—bread, peanut butter, jelly, and, of course, our well-worn map—within the copilot's reach. Nothing like a PB&J while cruising through a desert. We reset ourselves after last evening's failure to escape the town and, in a clean and reorganized car, embark again on our breakout plan. Amboy or bust.

Leaving Twentynine Palms we choose one of the many roads that displays signage to Amboy. You would think all roads lead to Amboy. Where are we, Rome? As we head east, we pass several signs with arrows pointing left that read "Amboy." We aren't buying it and remain focused on the road we have chosen. Before long, we see yet another sign, but this one points straight to Amboy. Only time will tell.

Nothing but open road and random adventures ahead of us.

We drive half an hour at top speed, then see another sign. Amboy is still ahead. Keep driving. There is a giant crater in the distance and nothing else as far as the eye can see, aside from tumbleweeds.

We finally pass a tiny sign, so small we almost miss it. (It might have been the size of a garage sale sign.) It reads "Amboy." I theorize it must be a precise GPS coordinate location rather than a town. We are very lucky we didn't attempt to find lodging here last night—we surely would have ended up camping in the crater.

Not too far ahead is said big crater and the town's only gas station and, apparently, its only lodging—Roy's Motel and Cafe. It is time for a bathroom break and a Coca-Cola.

Kristy and the gas pump; both high octane!

Continuing on, we begin to see signs for I-40, which will take us on the next leg of our journey; but we also see smaller signs on the same posts that read "Historic Route 66." We reach a fork in the road, left to I-40 and right to Historic Route 66.

Light bulb! I bet you can guess. One of our favorite movies is Cars. What can I say? You probably have figured out we're kids at heart by now. Our memory is about to serve us well; we learned in the film that Route 66 and I-40 are parallel, with I-40 bypassing towns and Route 66 running through them.

"Plan Some Spontaneity," a wine cork reads. It can't be planned sometimes, but it can be embraced. Road less traveled, here we come! Historic Route 66 is calling our names. This highway was one of the nation's first cross-country highways, originally stretching from Chicago to Los Angeles. The road itself was a fixture in popular culture references in the forties, fifties, and sixties.

Should we take the long way home? We have plenty of time, a voice in my head says.

"Hell yeah!" I respond to the voice out loud.

The winding road through the mountains adds to the adventure.

Feeling nostalgic as we drive Route 66, I hear Kristy's camera shutter non-stop. Of course, we sing the Route 66 song out loud.

"Get your kicks...on Route 66."

That is the only line we know, so we repeat it over and over. There is so much to see out the windows, and we imagine ourselves back in time seeing these iconic sights for the first time. That's not very hard to do because for us it is the first time we've been on this famous road.

A hidden gem of a town where jackasses roam free.

The highway turns curvy and mountainous, full of steep grades and sharp turns; and then, suddenly, the tiny town of Oatman, Arizona, appears, nestled in the foothills.

This is a jackass town, and that's not an insult. It's literal. There are jackasses everywhere. I find myself thinking that maybe the town was once full of me and my childhood friends because mom always said we were a bunch of jackasses. I guess we kind of liked that.

All the shops and souvenir stores are made of old timber; Oatman really has that Old West feel. We stop at an old gas station outside the town. It hasn't sold gas in at least half a century; instead, scattered on the lawn near the old pumps, are artifacts from the mining days. Another open-air museum! There is an old safe with the door open, probably left ajar on purpose to deter bandits. Farm equipment, forging tools and mining equipment are all on display, too.

Kristy and Johnny's 5 Fun Facts

1. Route 66 is America's most famous road.
2. It stretches 2,448 miles (3,940 km), from Chicago to Los Angeles.
3. It is also known as the Mother Road and America's Main Street.
4. It officially opened in 1926.
5. John Steinbeck's The Grapes of Wrath was inspired by his 1937 drive from Chicago to California.

Route 66 is no longer continuous and feeds us back into I-40 a few miles outside of Oatman. Kristy is disappointed that our nostalgic detour is over so soon. But before long we see more signs back to the Mother Road, and we don't hesitate at all this time. We take the exit and continue toward a town called Peach Springs, designated with the red tent icon on our map. As has become typical on this part of our trip, when we reach the town and ask about the campgrounds, we receive strange looks.

"Campgrounds?" they say, like we asked to see a donkey show or something. "Oh no, we don't have campgrounds here."

Meanwhile the barren horizon stretches out in every direction. I guess they just assume we'll pop our tent up anywhere and that is the norm.

As we approach the Hualapai Reservation, we fiddle with the radio dial and find a station playing Native American music. It is beautiful, complete with chants, drums, and flutes.

We imagine the Hollywood stars from the 50's and 60's traveling this stretch of road.

We crank it up and let it fill our ears and hearts as we drive through lovely grasslands. We imagine life hundreds of years ago and ourselves traveling by horseback at high speeds. Pretending to be on horses, we bounce up and down on the car seats as if in a gallop, holding invisible reins and laughing our asses off.

We decide to stop at whatever next town pops up instead of driving until sunset. Seligman has lots of shops and historic buildings to check out; and, for once, the little camping icons on our map are accurate. We find a campsite nearby at the KOA.

After we set up our tent, we ask the helpful KOA front desk woman for dining and photo op tips, then head out to explore the town. All the shops are charming; some of them clearly have supported this town since the fifties and sixties. We go to Westside Lilo's Cafe for dinner and it's great—KOA steered us right.

The sun is still up, but we go back to the tent to journal and plan

Route 66 is an amazing impromptu choice.

the next day's route. We're going to the Grand Canyon tomorrow. Which route will we take? We read our books and my mind wanders back to the bungalow in Rosarito, where a week earlier I was reading to Kristy. I begin to imagine what people did two hundred years ago in their living rooms with no technology, not even electricity. At night, light and warmth would come only from fireplaces, wood burning stoves, and lamps around dinner time. Hours after dinner were spent well with limited quantities of lamp oil to burn. Did they read to each other? Sing songs?

Play music? Write? I have a romantic notion that people who lived in this town—or places like it—sat near the fire telling stories. And I wonder: could I survive in a world like that after living in our world and becoming so used to instant gratification? Time must have moved more slowly then. I close my eyes and imagine.

Right before this trip, a cashier at Lowe's told me that two minutes was too long to wait in America these days. I was redeeming a gift card I got from an automated coin-counting machine when the cashier asked where I got the gift card. I told him about the coin counting machine and how it works.

"How long does it take to add up all those coins?" he asked.

"Oh, I don't know, maybe a couple of minutes?" I replied. "I guess it depends on how many coins."

"A couple of minutes? Hmm," he thought. "Two minutes is a long time to wait for anything in America these days."

"That's unfortunately true," I said.

I have to believe that years ago most people were far more patient; after all, it took ten minutes to boil water after a likely five-minute trek to retrieve it and twenty minutes for the stove to reach the right temperature. It was likely a two-minute hike to the chilly outhouse and probably took at least two minutes to grind coffee beans to make a cup of coffee. Imagine the difference in perspective on a two-minute timespan from today's world back to days of old. It makes me a bit sad to know humans are hesitant to try anything that may take too long.

The sun sets. It is time for bed since it is too windy for a campfire. I am not in the mood to prolong the night with battery-operated lights after imagining life in the Old West. We crawl into our sleeping bags and start an early night's rest.

We pose at many Route 66 signs as they are everywhere.

Day Fifteen
My Ass Hurts

"Keep your eyes on the stars, and your feet on
the ground."

—Theodore Roosevelt

May 15, 2017
Destination: Kanab, Arizona

Today's journey takes us to the South Rim of
the Grand Canyon. The landscape along the way
gradually changes from desert and grasslands
to forest and mountains. We stop at a gas station
for a restroom break and grab yogurt and fruit
for breakfast. We have plenty of bread left for
the sandwiches we'll make for our picnic lunch
later at the canyon. Back on the road, the tree

trunks become fat and the branches reach higher. As we near the canyon, traffic increases; SUVs and RVs fill the road close to the entrance.

Kristy and Johnny's 5 Fun Facts

1. The Grand Canyon was formed over a period of six million years by the Colorado River and is one of the most spectacular examples of erosion.
2. It won protective status as a national monument in 1908, after a visit by Theodore Roosevelt.
3. The park is 1,904 square miles (4,930 km).
4. Created in 1919, Grand Canyon National Park is a World Heritage Site located within Arizona.
5. The Grand Canyon is considered to be one of the Seven Natural Wonders of the World.

The views like this one at the Grand Canyon are awe inspiring.

Paper Maps, No Apps

It is such a clear day. Everything is perfect. Our only challenges are finding parking and avoiding all the selfie sticks. Some people have no concept of personal space—what we call "the bubble"—and time and again, as we're trying to take the perfect picture, out of nowhere someone bumps us aside to get his own. Even when we think we have waited for our turn, others around us have a different idea, and it's a big free for all. We line up the epic money shot and boom—someone walks right in and is forever planted in our photo album. This is a great day to practice patience.

TIP / Did you know: Selfie sticks are banned at all Disney Parks, Lollapalooza music festivals, Kentucky Derby, and many New York museums? That's just the top of the list. There are entire countries where they are banned.

We take a break from the crowds and find an out-of-the-way outdoor table for our picnic lunch and get cold spring water from a free fountain near the gift shop. Then we buy souvenirs, refill our water bottles, and drive to see the desert view from East Rim.

After enjoying the spectacular

Of course, the obligatory couples photo at the Grand Canyon.

View from bridge heading into Navajo Nation

This one reminds me of a Salvador Dali painting

views from East Rim, we gracefully retreat to the privacy of just us, in our car, on the road.

We head north toward Antelope Pass, looking for a little town at 8,700 feet elevation called Jacob Lake and hoping to find a campsite for the evening. No luck. The campground is full so we push on, and it is probably a good thing. It may have been too cold for our gear at that elevation.

Once again, we to drive into the evening without a place to stay. Any tension we might have felt in this situation early in our trip is gone now; we've had too many great adventures letting the fates guide us to worry! We don't even think of grabbing our phones to hunt for lodging. We just keep driving, eager for new experiences.

Soon we see signs for a city called Kanab; we recognize the name. We passed through this town on our way to Las Vegas via Zion National Park twelve days ago. It's a pretty big town, and we easily find a hotel—one with a sign in front that advertises a spa. At the front desk, we learn the spa is under construction, so the clerk gives us a nice discount instead; that will do. We unpack the car halfway, then decide to explore the town.

Kanab is a cute town with the usual Western souvenir shops and attractions. We stumble on a Hollywood gift shop with sets from old Western movies. Of course, Kristy makes me get in the jail cell for a prank photo to my mother.

A quick jail scene photo to play a joke on mom!

Dinnertime is near, and we are hungry. We don't anticipate any trouble finding a restaurant. There's one on the corner with a healthy number of cars outside, so we figure it must be popular. That is an understatement! When we get closer, we see the other five dozen cars parked out back.

There is an hour wait for a table for two. I guess it must be awful good. We're shocked any restaurant in this town has drawn such a crowd; the shop owners all mentioned it isn't peak tourist season. We put our names on the list, wait awhile, and get curious about the menu; so we ask for one to peruse. Then comes the real surprise.

I haven't seen prices like this since I was last in Vail, Colorado. They are through the roof! This place must be some kind of major chef's hideaway destination (and where do all these customers drive from?). We're not curious enough to learn more—in fact, prices like these begin to hurt my ass, right in the wallet area. We don't want to seem cheap, so we lie to the hostess.

"We're so sorry, our friends just texted us and they went to a different restaurant. Can you take our name off the waiting list? Thanks. Sorry. See you later."

We don't want to offend them—and later we kind of wish we had been more honest— "Your prices are absurd!"—but in the moment, stretching the truth seems the course to take.

"Do you think KFC is still open?" we wonder.

We walk a few blocks and find a cozy diner, complete with checkered tablecloths on Formica tables. Fried chicken dinner with buttermilk biscuits and picture perfect coleslaw send us back to the hotel satisfied and pain-in-the-ass-free.

Day Sixteen
See You on the Other Side

"The road is always better than the inn."
— Miguel de Cervantes Saavedra

May 16, 2017
Destination: Frisco, Colorado via Bryce Canyon

The morning of our last day on the road dawns and we awake confident that our smartphone-free travel experiment has been, for us, a great success. Kanab, Arizona, to Bryce Canyon is a short drive, and from Bryce Canyon it's a straight shot home on I-70.

We grab a quick breakfast and, with no temptation to turn on our phones, head out toward Bryce Canyon. It begins to snow a little

Even though it is Day 16, the smile is still present.

as we approach the national park. We pull into the gift shop parking lot to find no available parking spots; we have to wait for someone to leave. Who would have thought it would be this crowded on a cold, cloudy, snowy day?

A family emerges from the gift shop; we pull into their spot as soon as it's vacated and visit the shop. Kristy does her usual stocking up on gadgets, knickknacks, and collectible magnets; then we hop back in the car, eager to see the viewpoints. I have been to about twenty national parks, and Bryce ranks in my top three. I hope the photos can do it justice.

At the first lookout, we meet a group of guys from Salt Lake City who are very curious about the WEEDGALIZED.COM sticker on my rear windshield. It's not the first time this has happened, and, as usual, the discussion that follows about legalized marijuana is accompanied by laughter, many questions and an introduction to my book.

"Did you bring any gummies?" they ask. I shake my head and give them my business card, and we all smile.

We drive on to a few more lookouts, take our parting photos of this beautiful park, and it's soon time for the last leg of our journey.

Kristy and Johnny's 5 Fun Facts

1. Bryce Canyon National Park is actually not a canyon but a horseshoe shaped amphitheater carved from the eastern edge of the Paunsaugunt Plateau in Utah.
2. Erosion shaped the colorful limestone, sandstone, and mudstone into spires, pinnacles, mazes and fins known as hoodoos.
3. The Paiute Tribe described hoodoos as "red rocks standing like men in a bowl-shaped recess."
4. It became a national park on June 8, 1923.
5. Bryce is high in altitude with elevations of 8,000-9,000 feet (2,400-2,700 km)

We take a back road to the interstate and see very few cars. US 89 is as scenic as most of our trip has been. We stop to get ice cream in a tiny ice cream parlor in Circleville, Utah, the former home of Butch Cassidy, a billboard informs.

On I-70 west, it's cruise control and audio books until we arrive back in Frisco at our humble abode around 8:00 p.m., a little road weary but enriched by all the experiences.

The song on the radio as we finish our journey is "Tiny Dancer" by Elton John. The lyrics make me think.

"Count the headlights on the highway..."

I picture someone taking the time to gaze down a road and actually count headlights on the highway. The act seems relaxing to me, almost like a meditation. Or, maybe Bernie

Taupin had something else in mind when he wrote those lyrics; maybe he imagined a passenger in a moving car, counting each set of headlights as it passed. One thing is for sure: whether by the side of the road or in the car, you can't meditate on headlights if you're fixated on a smartphone.

Lessons from the road

Without smartphones, we felt a heightened sense of focus throughout our trip. Free to absorb all that was around us without distraction, we experienced each new adventure and each meaningful and chance encounter with friends and strangers much more deeply.

We also recognized the reason we take vacations is to get away—and that getting away means getting all the way away. Turn it off. Unplug. Disconnect. Decompress. Detox. Cleanse. Whatever you call it, it will be yours.

We've come to believe you're robbing yourself of the full experience of a road trip if you don't unplug. Road trips have a special impact on the soul. You feel like all the future lies literally in front of you when you're on the road, and the past is visible out the back windshield. The present is right where you are parked. It's a very linear feel everyone should experience at least once in a lifetime. There's nothing like it, and the possibilities are endless. The horizon holds adventures in every direction, waiting to unfold one at time.

On the road, in new and unfamiliar places, you often must rely on strangers and your ability to meet, greet, ask, learn, live, and share. I see these social skills in jeopardy with our technology addiction and reliance. I can so easily see a time when real world social interactions begin to feel like work, awkward and daunting. If that future becomes reality, we will have lost something very special about being human, because there is nothing as fulfilling as real connection.

See you on the other side!

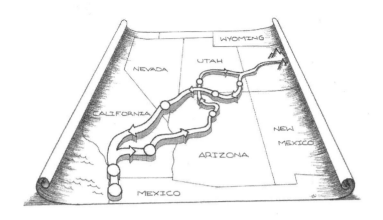

Day Seventeen
Unpacking Our Thoughts

"It's too late to just retreat to a quieter time."
—Sam Anderson

May 17, 2017
Destination: Living room to unpack

After our sixteen-day road trip, we resumed
our lives of mobile usage. We are human and
live in a technology-driven world. However,
our little social experiment did leave its mark.
We are aware of when, where, and how much
we lose ourselves in distraction technology. We
make a conscious effort not to over-consume,
especially when we spend time with other
people. We remind ourselves and each other

that people matter and deserve our focused attention.

What Lies Ahead?

Modern technology is much like a tsunami. Before it hits land, a tsunami pulls the tide back hundreds of feet, far past normal low tide boundaries; and then a series of smaller waves begin to roll in. They build quickly, and then the big wave hits: the nasty one, the one that can wreak havoc on and change landscapes and lives.

In this day and age, I think we are experiencing the small waves. One day, though, the big wave will break, and I'm not sure what that will mean. It feels like technology has us hypnotized, and it's only going to get worse. We're becoming more adept at being social online than we are face-to-face.

The tide pulled back in the era of inventions such as radio and television. The year 2007 was the turning point, when the small waves began to build. The iPhone was released, and awe-inspiring computer technology was placed into the palms of our hands. It's also the same year many companies unleashed social media platforms. Since then, each new wave comes faster and looms larger. I feel the monster wave coming and worry about what shape it will take and what it will do to us all.

Just like in the movie Invasion of the Body Snatchers, in the end all the humans eventually get snatched. I can hear Donald Sutherland's creepy scream now.

Results of an Over-technologized World

It is impossible to predict the future scenario. Will people feel more isolated? Does an isolated society lead to more conflict and large wars or increased suicide (which may be happening already)?

More people living through technology than the real world leads to sedentary, unhealthy lifestyles. The less people use the outdoors, the less they're inclined to protect it. Remember the pile of bicycles on the neighborhood's front lawns when inside wasn't an option? I can hear my parents now, "What are you doing in the house? Go play in the yard!"

Taking this trip and recording our experiences helped me become aware of how much I rely on modern technology. More importantly, it allowed me to revisit a time that wasn't as fast-paced and remember childhood joys like road trips, Hula-Hoops and Tastykakes.

It's made both Kristy and me try to use technology less in all aspects of our lives, beyond just our smartphones. We try to take the stairs instead of elevators, walk or ride our bikes to destinations within a few blocks instead of driving, pick up a newspaper or old book and sit and read every once in a while, and sometimes even bring that book along to help pass the time waiting in line at the DMV or post office.

Don't worry, I'm not going to say stop and smell the roses or listen to the birds sing, but if life feels like it's racing by too fast, you might want to make a few small changes. Sit and be idle. Start a coin collection. Play music. Listen to a song. Cook. Visit your local library. Take a nap in the middle of the day. Take a road trip with paper maps and get away, truly get away. Unplug for a while. And, OK, maybe smell a rose or two.

Johnny Bartender's Twisted Topics #1

"A dying culture invariably exhibits personal rudeness. Bad manners. Lack of consideration for others in minor matters. A loss of politeness, of gentle manners, is more significant than is a riot."
—Robert A. Heinlein, *Friday*

Our sixteen-day road trip is but one example of a conscious effort to reduce distraction technologies. You can enrich your life and detechnologize in other ways. Here are some of my favorites.

Top 10 Distraction Reduction Survival Tips

1. **He who plays, pays.** Play this game with your friends when you go out to dinner. Challenge everyone to place their phones in the middle of the table just as you sit down. The first to grab his phone and check it, for any reason, pays the bill.

2. **Ignore in the store.** Please, when approaching anyone working in customer service—front desk personnel, bank tellers, vendor booth attendants, grocery store clerks, retail employees, servers, bartenders, etc.—don't

text or talk on your phone. Be present. Chances are that person took care in getting ready for work: dressing nicely, shaving, applying makeup (or all of the above these days!). Notice that person. You don't have to engage in conversation, but at least make eye contact and smile. Be there for them as they are there for you.

3. **Be quiet.** Don't carry on loud phone conversations in public places (on buses, in grocery stores, etc.). Find a place out of the way to talk if it is vital. Remember, it is a phone not two cups on a string. You don't have to yell anymore.

4. **Exercise your body, not your phone.** Put all phones away in the gym! No texting, no calling, and (especially) no social media. Many people, including me, work out at a professional gym instead of at home to be inspired by others, and we're not inspired by watching you take a selfie. (Yes, it is evident you are updating your status, not changing your music, no matter what you tell us.)

5. **Prioritize your real-life relationships over your virtual ones.** When alone with your significant other, be present. Don't be a phubber.

6. **Make technology the scheduled exception.** Abide by scheduled times to check and utilize your device if your day involves being social, and allow yourself to

completely disconnect and recharge when on vacation.

7. **Walk away.** Take breaks often, and if you have to schedule breaks, do it.

8. **Preserve paper.** Try and incorporate physically reading a paper book.

9. **Mute the video!** When in a public place like a restaurant, bus, gym, etc., please don't blast the volume on videos you're showing your pals. Either keep it down or show them later, like in the car. If it's that crucial to your existence, carry headphones or earbuds.

10. **Remember, it wasn't always like this.** Try and imagine a time when life was slow. We don't need instant gratification. We're so impatient we stop the microwave with ten seconds left just to eat our chemical-filled frozen food faster. What are we doing with those ten seconds? More social media? Just food for thought.

Johnny Bartender's Twisted Topics #2
Join Our Community

We hope you've enjoyed our 16-day tech-free travel adventure. We met our goal to be technology-free 95 percent of our trip and had a blast doing it. Drop in at our website, johnnywelsh.com, where you'll find even more photos and video links to supplement the book. We love to keep in touch with all the fun and interesting people we meet along the way, so we plan to keep the adventure going over at johnnywelsh.com.

Happy trails from Johnny and Kristy!

Please visit us and share your smile photos on our site.

Johnny Bartender's Twisted Topics #3
Let's Mangia

Below is a list of the restaurants and curiosities we visited on our road trip.

Hole N" The Rock
11037 US Hwy. 191
Moab, UT 84532

The Dinosaur Museum
754 S. 200 W.
Blanding, UT 84511

The Bowl
24 N. Lake Powell Blvd.
Page, AZ 86040

Antelope Canyon X by Taadidiin Tours
MP 308 Hwy. 98 #3784
Page, AZ 86040

Guy Fieri's Vegas Kitchen
3535 Las Vegas Blvd S.
Las Vegas, NV 89109

Johnny Welsh

Peggy Sue's 50's Diner
35654 Yermo Rd.
Yermo, CA 92398

Betuccini's Pizzeria & Trattoria
Carretera Libre Tijuana-Ensenada Km 28.5
Paraiso Ortiz, 22710
Rosarito, BC, Mexico

Angus Bell Steakhouse (next door to Betuccini's)

Tapanco Restaurant
KM Blvd. Popotla 31
Popotla, 22710
Rosarito, BC, Mexico

Papas & Beer
Coronado 400
Playas Rosarito, 22710
Rosarito, BC, Mexico

Puerto Nuevo Restaurant
Blvd. Benito Juarez
Rosarito, BC, Mexico

Encinitas Ale House
1044 S. Coast Hwy. 101
Encinitas, CA 92024

Pipes Cafe
121 Liverpool Dr.
Cardiff, CA 92007

Paper Maps, No Apps

VG Donut & Bakery
106 Aberdeen Dr.
Cardiff, CA 92007

The Cardiff Office
110A Aberdeen Dr.
Cardiff, CA 92007

Best Pizza & Brew
102 Aberdeen Dr.
Cardiff, CA 92007

Pedro's Tacos
550 N. El Camino Real
San Clemente, CA 92672

Westside Lilo's Cafe
22750 US Hwy. 66,
Seligman, AZ 86337

The following restaurants are in Frisco, Colorado.
I bartend at both. If you happen to be passing
through, you might catch me here. I love to meet
fellow travelers and chat. Bring in your copy of
this book and I'd be happy to personalize it. My co-
workers all know where to find me, if I happen to
be off.

5th Ave. Grille
423 Main St.
Frisco, CO 80443

Johnny Welsh

Greco's Pastaria
311 E. Main St.
Frisco, CO 80443

Johnny Bartender's Twisted Topics #4
Stop Phubbing!

It has happened to all of us..

Phubbing
the rude social scourge of phone snubbing.
It means to interact with a mobile phone in preference to people in a social setting.

Don't you just hate it when someone snubs you by looking at their phone instead of paying attention?

The Stop Phubbing campaign group certainly does.

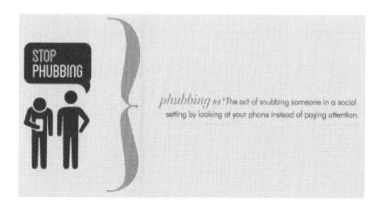

STOP PHUBBING

phubbing n) 'The act of snubbing someone in a social setting by looking at your phone instead of paying attention.

Melbourne university graduate Alex Haigh has created a campaign against bad mobile phone etiquette.

The Stop Phubbing campaign calls for victims to shame offenders by uploading photos onto to social media sites, write them letters, lay out anti-phubbing place cards at weddings and, for truly troublesome smartphone addicts, stage interventions.

Posters have been created for use in cafes, bars and restaurants, with slogans including "respect the food, the music and the company you are in", and "leave your phone in your pocket and have a chat in the real world". So please, join the campaign. Together, we can stamp out phubbing.

1. Go and vote | For or Against Phubbing
2. Stage a Phubbing Intervention | Send someone you know (who does it) an email to let them know their phubbing days are over
3. Download an Anti-Phubbing Poster | for your workplace
4. Download a Stop Phubbing Decal | for a venue you go to
5. Download a Wedding Place Card | if you're going to a wedding
6. Read 'When Not To Phub'

- www.stopphubbing.com

Do You Phub?
Don't worry, lots of people do, and are not aware they are doing it. If you don't think you do it,

see 25 Reasons We All Need To Stop Phubbing Each Other at BuzzFeed (link below)

Sources

- www.stopphubbing.com
- www.facebook.com/Stop.Phubbing
- www.buzzfeed.com
- Stop Phubbing

Phubbing | The End of Civilization As We know It

No TWEETING
No FACEBOOK
No INSTAGRAM
No FOURSQUARE
No SEXTING

RESPECT THE FOOD, THE MUSIC
AND THE COMPANY YOU'RE IN.

STOPPHUBBING.COM

Leave your

PHONE

IN YOUR
POCKET

AND HAVE A CHAT
IN THE REAL WORLD

STOPPHUBBING.COM

STOPPHUBBING.COM

You BELONG HERE,

YOUR PHONE *doesn't.*

Johnny Bartender's Twisted Topics #5
Are We Addicted?

The following are actual questionnaires developed by the Center for Internet and Technology Addiction's Founder Dr. David Greenfield. They are designed to help those addicted to their smartphones recognize their addiction. Take these tests and see where you stand. Be honest and be easy on yourself no matter what the results. Real change comes with awareness first, then action. It's okay to have fun with it. Look what we did with our road trip!

Smartphone Compulsion Test

1. Do you find yourself spending more time on your cell or smartphone than you realize?

☐ Yes
☐ No

2. Do you find yourself mindlessly passing time on a regular basis by staring at your cell or smartphone?

☐ Yes
☐ No

3. Do you seem to lose track of time when on your cell or smartphone?

☐ Yes
☐ No

4. Do you find yourself spending more time texting, tweeting or emailing as opposed to talking to people in person?

☐ Yes
☐ No

5. Has the amount of time you spend on your cell or smartphone been increasing?

☐ Yes
☐ No

6. Do you wish you could be a little less involved with your cell or smartphone?

☐ Yes
☐ No

7. Do you sleep with your cell or smartphone (turned on) under your pillow or next to your bed regularly?

☐ Yes
☐ No

8. Do you find yourself viewing and answering texts, tweets and emails at all hours of the day and night—even when it means interrupting

other things you are doing?

☐ Yes
☐ No

9. Do you text, email, tweet or surf while driving or doing other similar activities that require your focused attention and concentration?

☐ Yes
☐ No

10. Do you feel your use of your cell or smartphone decreases your productivity at times?

☐ Yes
☐ No

11. Do you feel reluctant to be without your cell or smartphone, even for a short time?

☐ Yes
☐ No

12. Do you feel ill-at-ease or uncomfortable when you accidentally leave your smartphone in the car or at home, have no service or have a broken phone?

☐ Yes
☐ No

13. When you eat meals, is your cell or smartphone always part of the table place setting?

☐ Yes
☐ No

14. When your cell or smartphone rings, beeps or buzzes, do you feel an intense urge to check for texts, tweets, emails, updates, etc.?

☐ Yes
☐ No

15. Do you find yourself mindlessly checking your cell or smartphone many times a day, even when you know there is likely nothing new or important to see?

☐ Yes
☐ No

Disclaimer: It should be noted that no medical or psychiatric diagnosis can be made solely by a written test or screening instrument alone; this survey is intended for educational and informational purposes only. If you score is on the higher side it would be reasonable to examine whether your use or over-use is creating any problems in work-life balance. If you are concerned about your Smartphone use, you may wish to consult with a mental health/addiction professional with expertise in Internet and Technology Addiction (Process/Behavioral Addictions).

Digital Distraction Test

Are You Too Connected?

Take our Digital Distraction Test; a simple 12 item quiz to see if you are suffering from Digital Distraction and you could use an aid to your Digital Digestion. Our short quiz may help you see if you are a bit too digitally connected and that you might connect with your world better by disconnecting from your devices some of the time! The Digital Distraction Test may be the reminder you need to "Plug Back into Life!"

1. Do you find yourself spending more and more time online or on your digital devices (computer, laptop, tablet or Smartphone) than you realize.

☐ Yes
☐ No

2. Do you find yourself mindlessly passing time on a regular basis by staring at your Smartphone, Tablet, or Computer even when there might be better or more productive things to do? And do you seem to lose track of time when on any of these devices?

☐ Yes
☐ No

3. Do you find yourself spending more time with 'virtual friends' as opposed to real people nearby?

☐ Yes
☐ No

4. Has the amount of time you spend on your digital devices and the Internet been increasing?

☐ Yes
☐ No

5. Do you secretly wish you could be a little less wired or connected to your devices such as your Smartphone laptop, tablet Internet, etc.?

☐ Yes
☐ No

6. Do you sleep with your Smartphone ON under your pillow or next to your bed regularly?

☐ Yes
☐ No

7. Do you find yourself viewing and answering texts, tweets, and emails at all hours of the day and night—even when it means interrupting other things you are doing?

☐ Yes
☐ No

8. Do you Text, Email, Tweet or Surf while driving or doing other similar activities that require your focused attention and concentration?

☐ Yes
☐ No

9. Do you feel your use of technology actually decreases your productivity at times?

☐ Yes
☐ No

10. Do you find yourself feeling somewhat ill-at-ease or uncomfortable when you accidentally leave your phone or other Internet digital device in the car or at home, if you have no service, or if it is broken?

☐ Yes
☐ No

11. Do you feel reluctant to be without your Smartphone or other digital devices, even for a short time; when you leave the house you ALWAYS have your Smartphone or other digital device with you?

☐ Yes
☐ No

12. When you eat meals is your Smartphone always part of the table place setting?

☐ Yes
☐ No

Disclaimer: It should be noted that no medical or psychiatric diagnosis can be made solely by a written test or screening instrument alone; this survey is intended for educational and informational purposes only. If you score is on the higher side it would be reasonable to examine whether your use or over-use is creating any problems in work-life balance. If you are concerned about your Smartphone use, you may wish to consult with a mental health/addiction professional with expertise in Internet and Technology Addiction (Process/ Behavioral Addictions).

Twelve Warning Signs of Internet Addiction in Your Spouse, Friend or Loved One

Recognizing the warning signs of Internet addiction in your spouse or loved one is the first step in your helping them help themselves. The following warning signs should serve as general guidelines for you to determine whether or not your spouse, family member or friend may have a problem.

Does your loved one:

1. Spend a lot of time alone with their computer or smartphone on a regular basis?
2. Become defensive when you confront them with their behavior?
3. Seem either unaware of what they have been doing, or attempt to deny it?
4. Prefer spending time with their device or on the Internet rather than with other people?
5. Lose interest in other, previously important activities, e.g., friends, sports, work, hobbies, exercise, etc.?

6. Appear to be more socially isolated, moody or irritable?

7. Seem to be establishing "a second life," with new and different friends whom they met online?

8. Spend greater amounts of time online, and attempt to cover or "minimize" the screen or hide the phone when you come in the room.

9. Talk about their time on the computer incessantly, and seem to draw meaning in their life from this activity.

10. Exhibit signs that their work or school performance is suffering; perhaps they were fired, grades are slipping or their household responsibilities are neglected.

11. Talk about their time on the computer incessantly and seem to draw meaning in their life from this activity.

12. Have legal problems as a result of their Internet behavior,e.g., the loss of child custody, divorce, or sexual harassment charges at work due to downloading pornography, etc.

Disclaimer: It should be noted that no medical or psychiatric diagnosis can be made solely by a written test or screening instrument alone; this survey is intended for educational and informational purposes only. If you score is on the higher side it would be reasonable to examine whether your use or over-use is creating any problems in work-life balance. If you are concerned about your Smartphone use, you may wish to consult with a mental health/addiction professional with expertise in Internet and Technology Addiction (Process/ Behavioral Addictions).

Johnny Bartender's Twisted Topics #6
Apps for No Apps

Six apps to help stop using apps (or, at least, reduce the most time consuming apps):

1. Offtime (iOS, Android)-Blocks apps like Facebook and games
2. Moment (iOS)-tracks usage and will establish limits for smartphone usage
3. BreakFree (iOS, Android)-has standard tracking features and will show users their level of addiction
4. Flipd (iOS, Android)-a more aggressive approach by locking smartphones for a set time
5. AppDetox (Android)-allows users to set times for apps when they won't be a disruption
6. Stay on Task (Android)-reminds users to stay on track with tasks at hand

Smart Pledge

Make a promise to yourself to be aware of how often and when you are using your phone, with the goal of being attentive to those who you come into contact with in a casual manner—post office staff, retail employees, servers, bartenders, bankers, etc.—as well as those you have meaningful relationships with at home and in the community. Take our Low-Tech Challenge over at JohnnyWelsh.com.

Acknowledgements
For Mom and Dad

Once the travel bug bites, you may be infected
the rest of your life...

First and foremost I could not have written this
book without Kristy Marie Smith, my girlfriend
in this book and now fiancée. Her trusty camera
and keen eye have captured these wonderful
memories.

I must give praise, love, and
acknowledgement to my mom and dad for the
sacrifices they made to ensure I received a good
education.

It takes a team to produce a book and I have
been very fortunate to meet some of the best in
the industry. Jody Rein, Nick Zelinger, Kathy
Meis and the Bublish team have all played
crucial roles on this project from consulting to
editing to design.

I am also fortunate to have amazing friends.
Elle Malone spent countless hours sketching and
re-sketching the illustrations.

Thank you to all the players: Hannah,
Jeremy, Jason, Jacqueline, Zack, Paul, Christina,
Neal, CJ, Johnny Day, Gunner, Mark, Max, Horse,

Johnny Welsh

Matt da Ritt, David Sedaris, random customs agents, Big Mike, Bello, Britteny, and Laura

Thank you to the peer review readers: CJ, Neal, Erica, Paige

Special thanks to AAA for the amazing paper maps.

About the Author

Johnny Welsh has worked as a professional bartender in Frisco, Colorado, for over twenty years. When he's not slinging drinks, he spends his time twisting bar topics into books. In addition to Paper Maps: No Apps, he's the author of the award-winning Weedgalized in Colorado: True Tales From the High Country, which is the good, the bad, and the funny about legalizing marijuana in Colorado.

If you enjoyed this book or it helped you, please leave a review help spread the movement.

Speaking engagements on a variety of topics can be booked through his website: writing, bartending, travel, cannabis culture, living a low-tech life, and more

Contact:
Weedgalized@yahoo.com
Peak 1 Publishing, LLC
PO Box 2046
Frisco, CO 80443

Bibliography

Alter, Adam. "'Irresistible' by Design: It's
    No Accident You Can't Stop Looking at the
    Screen." Interview by Terry Gross. Fresh Air,
    NPR, March 13, 2017. Audio, 30:20. https://
    www.npr.org/templates/transcript/transcript.
    php?storyId=519977607.

Alter, Adam. *Irresistible: The Rise of Addictive
    Technology and the Business of Keeping Us
    Hooked.* New York: Penguin Press, 2017.
    Benedictus, Leo. "Chinese city opens
    'phone lane' for texting pedestrians." The
    Guardian, September 15, 2014. https://www.
    theguardian.com/world/shortcuts/2014/
    sep/15/china-mobile-phone-lane-distracted-
    walking-pedestrians.

Carr, Nicholas G. *The Shallows: What the
    Internet is Doing to Our Brains.* New York: W.
    W. Norton & Company, 2010.

Center for Internet and Technology Addiction,
    The. Accessed November 30, 2018. http://
    virtual-addiction.com/.

Donner, Richard, dir. *The Goonies.* 1985.
    Burbank, CA: Warner Home Video, 1986.
    VHS. DK Travel. *DK Eyewitness Travel Guide:*
    Southwest USA & National Parks. New York:
    DK Eyewitness Travel, 2016.

Fodor's. *The Official Guide to America's National*
    Parks. 13th ed. New York: Fodor's Travel
    Publications, 2008.

Goldman, Jeremy. "Six Apps to Stop Your
    Smartphone Addiction." Inc., October
    21, 2015. https://www.inc.com/jeremy-
    goldman/6-apps-to-stop-your-smartphone-
    addiction.html.

Heckerling, Amy, dir. *Fast Times at Ridgemont*
    High. 1982. Universal City, CA: Universal
    Pictures Home Entertainment, 2011. DVD.

John, Elton. *Madman Across the Water.* DJM
    Records DJLPH 420, 1971, LP.

Kaufman, Philip, dir. *Invasion of the Body*
    Snatchers. 1978. Beverly Hills, CA: MGM
    Home Entertainment, 1998. DVD.

Kiersch, Fritz, dir. *Children of the Corn.* 1984.
    Beverly Hills, CA: Anchor Bay Entertainment,
    2001. DVD.

Lasseter, John and Joe Ranft, dir. Cars. 2006. Burbank, CA: Buena Vista Home Entertainment, 2006. DVD.

Ma, Alexandra. "German Company Installs Lights Along Curbs For Pedestrians Glued To Their Phones." *Huffington Post*, April 26, 2016. https://www.huffingtonpost.com/entry/germany-stadtwerke-augsburg-ground-traffic-light-smartphone_us_571f967de4b0b49df6a91b5e

McRae, W. C., and Judy Jewell. *Moon Zion and Bryce*. Lebanon: Moon Travel, 2008.

Myrick, Daniel and Eduardo Sanchez, dir. *The Blair Witch Project*. Santa Monica, CA: Artisan Entertainment, 1999. DVD.

Orwell, George. *Nineteen Eighty-Four*. London: Penguin Publishing Group, 1950.

Reiner, Robert, dir. *Stand by Me*. 1986. Culver City: CA: RCA/Columbia Home Pictures Video, 1987. DVD.

Scott, Ridley, dir. *Thelma & Louise*. 1991. Beverly Hills, CA: MGM Home Entertainment, 2004. DVD.

Serafian, Richard C., dir. *Vanishing Point*. 1971.
Los Angeles, CA: Twentieth Century Fox
Home Entertainment, 2004. DVD.

Spielberg, Steven, dir. *Jaws*. 1975. Universal
City, CA: Universal Studios Home Video, 2000.
DVD.

Stanton, Andrew, dir. *Wall·E*. Burbank, CA:
Walt Disney Studios Home Entertainment,
2008. DVD. "Stop Phubbing." Only Australia.
Accessed November 30, 2018. https://www.
onlyaustralia.com.au/issues/stop-phubbing/.

Printed in Great Britain
by Amazon